English # Heritage

Book of

Flag Fen

Prehistoric Fenland Centre

English ⌗ Heritage
Book of
Flag Fen
Prehistoric Fenland Centre

Francis Pryor

B. T. Batsford Ltd/English Heritage
London

This book is dedicated to
the Flag Fen students, volunteers
and professionals

First published 1991.

Typeset by Lasertext Ltd,
Stretford, Manchester
and printed in Great Britain by
The Bath Press, Avon

Published by B. T. Batsford Ltd
4 Fitzhardinge Street, London W1H 0AH

A CIP catalogue record for this book is
available from the British Library

ISBN 0 7134 6752 5 (cased)
0 7134 6753 3 (limp)

Contents

Illustrations

Colour plates

1

The Fens: A fair spot and goodly

Peterborough is a bustling, modern city of extraordinary vigour and with an unrivalled ancient past. Nowadays the city owes its success to modern communications: principally the Great North Road (the A1) and the main London to Edinburgh railway line. In remoter years, however, the region's prosperity depended to a large part on the Fens. To outsiders this was a region of mire, marsh-gas and disease, but to those who actually lived there it was a land of extraordinary richness and diversity; so let the splendid words of the twelfth-century chronicler Hugh Candidus set the scene:

> Now Burch [Peterborough] is situate in the region of Gyrwas [the Fens], because the same fen begins there on the eastern side, extending for sixty miles or more. The same is very valuable to men because there are obtained in abundance all things needful for them that dwell thereby, logs and stubble for kindling, hay for the feeding of their beasts, thatch for the roofing of their houses, and many other things of use and profit, and moreover it is very full of fish and fowl. There are divers rivers and many other waters there, and moreover great fishponds. In all these things that district is very rich. So this Burch is built in a fair spot, and a goodly, because on the one side it is rich in fenland, and in goodly waters, with many fertile meads and pastures, and on the other it has abundance of ploughlands and woodlands, with many fertile meads and pastures. On all sides it is beautiful to look upon and easy to approach on foot, save only on the eastern side where there is no coming to it save in a boat.

This book is mainly concerned with Hugh's 'eastern side', land today occupied by roads and factories; in the distant past, however, it saw a succession of ancient farms, villages and hamlets. The region is now known as Peterborough's Eastern Industrial Area, but until recently it retained its Norse name of Fengate, or 'road leading to the fen'. About 800 m ($\frac{1}{2}$ mile) east of Fengate, in the peaty landscape that was flooded until very recently, sits the superbly-preserved site of Flag Fen. In the following pages we will attempt to reconstruct life in Fengate from the beginnings of farming in the Neolithic period (c.4500BC) until the widespread flooding of the later Roman period (c. AD 300).

There must be a tendency, when writing about nearly twenty years' work in one place, to become very possessive and to think in terms of the first person singular. But I must emphasize that both Fengate and Flag Fen are, and were, team efforts; the teams were usually quite small – perhaps six to eight people – reaching a maximum in mid-summer of about fourteen to eighteen in all. Within the evolving teams were key specialists, many of whom still keep in touch with the project, and whose work will be discussed in the appropriate places below. Having said that, the fact remains that I have become personally very involved with the sites; doubtless this means that I am unable to take a disinterested or dispassionate view, but I do not think that this matters particularly. It is a myth to suppose that any archaeologist can remove him or herself from their work and I see little fault in admitting this from the outset.

1 *Map of the Fens. (Martin Redding.)*

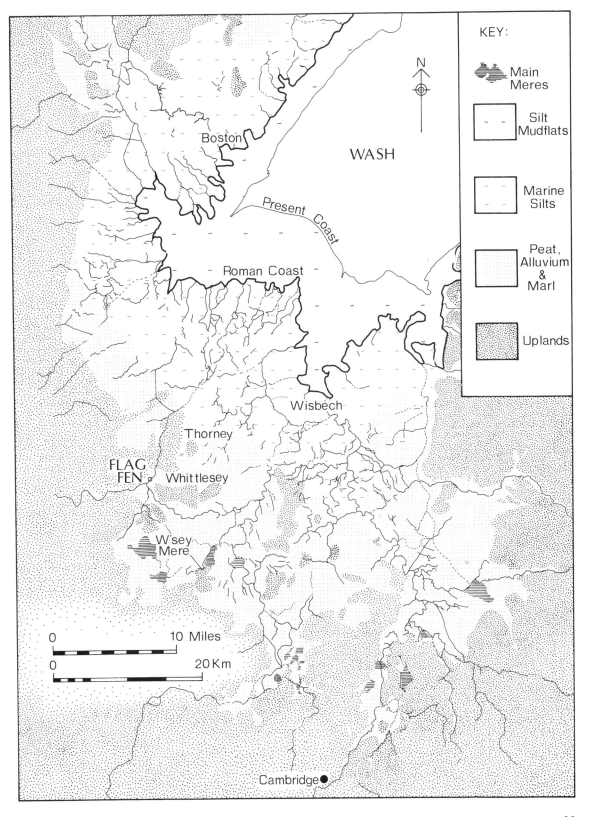

2 *Modern Fenland view near Whittlesey, Cambs.*

It would be impossible to reconstruct ancient life without also attempting to rebuild the ancient landscape too – as people had to live out their lives within an actual physical environment. Given Peterborough's location at the extreme edge of the wetlands, a discussion of the Fens is essential. The Fens were once Britain's largest and most diverse wetland; estimates of size vary, but 400,000 ha (1 million acres) is a widely accepted figure. Most of the land lies below the 4 m (12½ ft) contour, although higher 'islands' protrude above it in places.

The Fen landscape

The flat Fenlands of East Anglia and south Lincolnshire were once Britain's largest wetland (1). The pre-Roman Fen was a country of reeds, willow sedge and wildfowl, of biting winter winds and abundant fish and fowl. Today the land is very different: huge fields of wheat and sugarbeet are separated by dead straight dykes with no trees to fill the emptiness around (2). The sky itself is part of this landscape; surely, no other place can demonstrate so clearly why the ancients considered the heavens a vast dome. Some would see this landscape as flat and monotonous; Fenmen think that any fool can appreciate a hill.

The Fen landscape may appear flat and featureless to the visitor from outside, but in reality it is as varied as anywhere in Britain: in a flat landscape the smallest prominences can acquire a very special significance, in a wet season a rise of just a few centimetres can make the difference between life and death. It is not for nothing that Fen folk have always had a keen eye for topography.

We will see below how the Fens were 'tamed' from being a watery landscape to one in which the farmer reigns supreme, and there can be little doubt that this 'taming' process has rid Fenland of much of its mystery and romance. Nevertheless the region has an atmosphere of its own. It takes someone who knows the Fens and lives there to write about it properly. Dorothy Sayers is a fine example of a good Fen writer; she captures the feel of the place with absolute topographical precision. This is illustrated by her description, from *The Nine Tailors*, of Bunter driving Lord Peter Wimsey across the deep Fen to the higher 'Marshland' country around Wisbech ('Walbeach': like all her names, authentic-sounding but non-existent). The book is set between the wars, hence the reference to pumping windmills which have all, sadly, vanished.

Mile after mile the flat road reeled behind them. Here a windmill, there a solitary farmhouse, there a row of poplars strung along the edge of a reed-grown dyke. Wheat, potatoes, beet, mustard and wheat again... A long village street with a grey and ancient church tower, a red-brick chapel, and the vicarage set in a little oasis of elm and horse-chestnut, and then once more dyke and windmill, wheat mustard and grassland. And as they went, the land flattened more and more, if a flatter flatness were possible, and the windmills became more numerous, and on the right hand the silver streak of the Wale River came back into view, broader now, swollen with the water of the Thirty-foot and of Harper's Cut and St Simon's Eau, and winding and spreading here and there, with a remembrance of its ancient leisure. Then, ahead of the great circle of the horizon, a little bunch of spires and roofs and a tall tree or so, and beyond them the thin masts of shipping. And so, by bridge and bridge the travellers came to Walbeach, once a great port, but stranded now far inland with the silting of the marshes and the choking of the Wale outfall...

Before we become wholly swamped in mist and mystery we should consider how and when the Fens formed. The principle is simple: about 10,000 years ago the climate grew milder and meltwater from the Ice Age ice-fields flowed into the world's oceans, causing global sea levels to rise. Obviously the first areas to feel the effects of these changes were low-lying, and the North European plain, now occupied by the North Sea was one such area. River valleys flooded first and were enlarged into bays, such as the Wash. The Fens are in fact a large natural depression that was not quite deep enough to be permanently inundated by the

North Sea. Instead, the area began to get wet in its lowest-lying river valleys around 7000 BC, at which point peats started to form. Thereafter the area was flooded by the sea during storm tides, or by rivers bursting their natural banks when in spate.

These processes commenced very approximately between 7000 and 3000 BC, depending on how low-lying was the land. Peterborough sits on the western or inland edge of the Fens and is relatively high by Fenland standards; its fens therefore flooded quite late. Just east of Peterborough, at one of the highest points of the true Fens, the land beneath Flag Fen did not become permanently waterlogged until sometime around 2000 or 1500 BC (the precise date is something we are still actively trying to work out). What were the general effects of these flooding processes or episodes? The first thing to emphasize is that they were complex and require much unravelling; what follows is a simplified version of the true story.

We could do worse than borrow Dorothy Sayers' literary device and make an imaginary journey across the varied soils of Fenland, starting at Wisbech, near the Wash, and heading inland, towards Peterborough and the dryland of what was once mainland Britain.

The 'Marshland' countryside around Wisbech is the only part of Fenland that feels old: there are trees and hedges, lanes meander and massive medieval churches dominate the dispersed hamlets; as such it can hardly be considered as typical of Fenland at all. The silt soils are all of marine origin and are extraordinarily productive for the farmer. The Marshland landscape need not detain the prehistorian long, as the silts that form it were mainly laid down by marine floods in the later Iron Age, consequently prehistoric (pre-Roman) finds are very rare indeed.

West of Marshland we move into a more open landscape of heavier clay and silt soils interrupted by raised banks of silt known locally as 'roddons' or 'rodhams'. These raised banks wander across the landscape in a seemingly aimless fashion, but when viewed from the air they can be seen to form immensely elaborate branching patterns (see **14**). Their precise interpretation is still a matter for debate, but they are undoubtedly the remains of marine water courses, and probably tidal creeks, dating from a time when the North Sea covered large parts of south Lincolnshire and

Cambridgeshire. When the creeks were active they flowed through a landscape of peats and peaty clays. The water in them flowed along carrying a heavy load of suspended silts; when the tide turned, the water stopped moving and dumped its suspended load on the creek bed. Over the years the material built up and sometimes the creek actually blocked up; occasionally the remains of the old stream channel are still visible, usually showing up as a thin dark line on an aerial photo, wending its way down the centre of the silty creek. After drainage, the lighter soils through which the creek had cut its course would tend to 'shrink' as the peats dried out, leaving the heavier material in the creek beds to project above the ground surface they had once flowed through. The reversal of the landscapes' original contours – where what was once high is now low, and vice versa – often makes the reconstruction and interpretation of lost Fenland landscapes very difficult indeed.

The soils of Marshland essentially derived from the North Sea, but the Fen country immediately inland, to the south and west, is far more complex: the roddons are plainly marine, but the land around them can derive from a number of sources: earlier spreads of sea-borne silts, river-borne (alluvial) clays or peats – some formed locally, others washed-in from elsewhere. In places, especially east of the old 'island' at Thorney, there is evidence for substantial marine inundations (or transgressions) in the Bronze Age, around 1000 BC; these inundations are now thought to be part of a long-continuing process that became more severe at certain times and in certain places. Like the Iron Age transgression nearer the Wash, the Bronze Age floods laid down huge spreads of silt. The Bronze Age silts can generally be distinguished from those of the Iron Age that followed because they are finer textured, darker and more clay-like. Having said that, I defy anyone to date silts near the landward edge of Marshland; the picture is simply too complex for any precision. All one can say with assurance is that they were laid down by the sea before the Roman Conquest.

Moving even further inland we come to the earliest Fenland marine transgression. Like those of the Iron and Bronze Ages the so-called Fen Clay transgressions probably consisted of many smaller floods spread over perhaps a thousand years or more. Dating is still highly problematical but there is now accumulating evidence to suggest that the Fen Clay transgressions of the southern Fens, north of Cambridge, are considerably earlier than those east of Peterborough; the former probably started shortly after 3000 BC, the latter seem to have been taking place around 1800–1500 BC. There seems to be no good reason to suppose that there was a gap between the two sets of flooding which are essentially manifestations of the same phenomenon, only displaced in time and space, the episodes of flooding moving from one region to another.

The Fen Clay itself is widespread and very straightforward to identify as it has a characteristic soft-soap or greasy feel, and distinctively mottled appearance – hence its description in some older literature as the Buttery Clay. Today we are prevented from using the simple term 'Fen Clay' and are supposed instead to refer to the soil scientists' polysyllabic 'Barroway Drove Beds'. Similarly the Bronze Age transgression deposits are known as 'Younger Barroway Drove Beds', whereas the Iron Age silts of Marshland are now 'Terrington Beds'. These terms are for specialists and I avoid them whenever I can.

So to sum up, had I been writing this book ten years ago, it would have been possible to offer a more straightforward picture, but the long series of radiocarbon dates now available have shown conclusively how very complex the situation is. Whenever the sea was not flooding the region, the countryside remained as flat and wet as ever: far inland, the low-lying ground east of Huntingdon and Peterborough, but north of Cambridge, received freshwater from the rivers Nene and Ouse, which debouched into the Fenland basin at this point. Once within the basin these great rivers generally had a central course, marked by a massive silt roddon, but there were also hundreds of smaller, subsidiary courses which flooded every winter to lay down thin sheets of flood-clay over huge areas around the Fen margins. These river-borne flood clays often contained peats washed-in from peatbeds further upstream. The very edges of the Fen also hid small bays and inlets in which peats could grow, unaffected by the laying-down of the river-borne clays.

So the net effect of the various episodes of marine flooding interspersed with peat growth was to build up a sedimentary 'layer cake'. The bowl, as it were, was usually provided by

3 *The Holme Fen Post. The top of this post was level with the ground surface around 1850; since then the land has 'shrunk' due to drainage.*

the underlying rocks of the Fen Basin: solid geological strata of Jurassic or Cretaceous age. Then, as conditions became wetter, peats were laid down; these lower peats were overlain by Fen Clay; then there was more peat growth, followed by another series of marine floods (Bronze Age), yet more peat and then the final,

massive (Iron Age) marine transgression. So-called 'upper peats' would form above and below the silts of the Bronze Age and Iron Age transgressions.

This, at least, is the general picture around Peterborough which I have simplified enormously. It used to be thought that a similar picture applied throughout Fenland, but recent research has shown this not to be the case: instead each region has its own sequence of deposits that can only be cross-correlated with difficulty. When taken as a whole, however, the succession Lower Peat – Fen Clay – Upper Peat – Marine Silt is quite consistent over large stretches of Fenland. It is only the dates that change from place to place.

Fens and bogs are not just different words for the same thing: each is a very distinctive environment with its own characteristic plants and animals. Bogs can develop from Fens if conditions remain wet and stable for long enough, but they are more commonly found in areas of high rainfall, such as Ireland and Lancashire. Fens generally form in wetlands fed by groundwater which is often rich in lime and other mineral nutrients. The plants are usually far larger than in bogs and include many species of wet-loving trees, shrubs, reeds, rushes and so on. By and large the ecology of a fen is fairly robust and resilient, and unlike bogs can tolerate the activities of man (except-ing, of course, wholesale drainage) without too much resentment. Once cleared of tree cover, for instance, a fen can be managed for hay and grazing – or indeed for reed and sedge for thatching, as at the modern nature reserve at Wicken Fen, near Ely. Fen peat, however, is less sought-after for fuel than the finer-textured *Sphagnum* mosses of bogs. Having said that, there is abundant evidence for the cutting of fen peats in Norfolk and north-west Cambridge-shire and of course the Norfolk Broads owe their very existence to medieval peat-cutting. The Broads, incidentally, are a rare example where man's over-exploitation of the environ-ment has had a largely beneficial effect – although pleasure craft and general pollution are now undoing much of that good.

The largest body of freshwater in England was once not Windermere, as today, but, prior to its draining around 1850, was located immediately south of the small market town of Whittlesey, which sits on its own natural clay island just to the east of Peterborough. Whittle-sey Mere was reputed to be no deeper than 2 m (6½ ft) but it illustrates well the sort of closed freshwater environment that could be found along the fringe of the Fen-edge. Despite the chalky, lime-rich waters of the Nene which passed by its northern boundary, Whittlesey Mere was able to sustain an acid-loving 'raised bog' environment in which *Sphagnum* mosses and other lime-hating plants thrived. The *Sphagnum* mosses of the 'raised bog' formed a huge dome-like mound which was sufficiently large to keep the marine waters of the Fen

Clay inundations at bay: on air photos it is noticeable that Fen Clay roddons never quite reach as far west as the old Mere. Outside Whittlesey Mere and one or two other areas that were naturally sheltered from lime-rich water, the low-lying freshwater wetlands of the southern and western Fens supported a more typical fen vegetation, characterized by willow and alder trees, shrubs such as guelder rose or buckthorn and a huge variety of marginal and aquatic herbs, such as reeds, rushes, sedges, pondweeds and water lilies.

The undulating marshy zone at the very landward edge of Fenland is difficult to map with any precision: where the ground is sloping steeply the transition from fen to dryland is likely to be quite sharp, but in the Peterborough area the slope is almost negligible and the boundary between wet and dry at any given time is very hard to pin down. This discussion will therefore be deferred until the next chapter, where the surroundings of Fengate and Flag Fen are described in greater detail.

Fenland drainage

The draining of the Fens has traditionally been put forward as an account of man's victory over nature. More recently, attitudes have changed, especially among people who actually live in Fenland: many of us rarely see water from one day to another, yet we all have serious doubts about the future, if sea levels continue to rise and if the greenhouse effect really does begin to bite, then will our houses remain above water in, say, twenty years time? Today we live in an over-drained, ecologically sterile fen landscape, but there is always the danger of catastrophic flooding.

It is sometimes said that the Romans first drained the Fens. This is not true. The last two or three centuries before Christ had witnessed massive marine transgressions around the Wash that laid down the Iron Age silts of Marshland. This period of increased marine activity was followed by one of relative tran-quillity in which settlements and salt-extrac-tion sites of the early Roman period (first and second centuries AD) appeared on the higher Iron Age silts and natural islands. These set-tlers were probably not actual immigrants from Rome, but local 'native' British families, sup-plemented perhaps by a few retired soldiers from abroad. It must also be said, however, that some archaeologists are of the opinion that

Fenland was part of a huge Imperial Roman estate, largely inhabited by military veterans and their families. I have to say, however, that I find this notion rather odd. The Romano-British colonists were simply taking advantage of favourable natural conditions and when ground water levels rose again in the third century AD, they moved on.

The early post-Roman use of the Fens was restricted, largely because of wetness, but the recent Fenland Survey has found much evidence for later Saxon and Saxo-Norman exploitation of the Fen and its margins. Again, the Saxon settlement of Fenland seems to have been largely opportunistic, although David Hall (of the Fenland Survey) has convincingly suggested there was large-scale settlement of the wetlands west of Wisbech, which were embanked and drained for the purpose.

Medieval communities by and large carried out piecemeal drainage of marginally wet land;

there was no large-scale attempt at drainage or flood-prevention, apart from Bishop Morton's extraordinary and pioneering canalization of the River Nene north of Whittlesey in the late fifteenth century.

The main drainage of the Fens is a story that has been definitively described by Professor Darby in his book, *The Drainage of the Fens* (1948), and more recently in his *The Changing Fenland* (1983). The early drainage work took place before and after the English Civil War and was master-minded by the great engineer Cornelius Vermuyden. Vermuyden realized the water from the uplands around the Fens had to be taken across the Fen basin as quickly as possible and its outfall into the sea had to be clear and unimpeded. Never before had anyone in Britain attempted to drain so large an area of peatland as the southern Fens; Vermuyden achieved this by diverting the waters of the River Ouse into an entirely new channel, the Old Bedford River. This ameliorated the flooding to a great extent, but after the Civil War the old problems resumed and yet another massive channel was constructed alongside the

4 *Mechanized dyke dredging near Parson Drove, Cambs.*

Old Bedford River – the New Bedford River. Even today, when conditions become particularly wet, and water cannot readily be released into the North Sea, the land between the two Bedford rivers – known as washland – is deliberately flooded and acts as a temporary holding reservoir.

Fenmen have a reputation, probably unjustified, for being fierce; locally, indeed, they are known as 'Fen Tigers'. In the early seventeenth century, as the wetland began to be tamed, they complained vociferously and sabotaged dykes, sluices and other works of the gentlemen 'improvers'. It is hard not to sympathize with them, for their traditional independent way of life was being destroyed. Their fishing and fowling grounds were taken over by sheep and cattle, while seasonally flooded common land and turbaries (peat-cutting lands) were drained and given to other people, often from outside the area.

The history of the last three hundred years

of Fen drainage is essentially a race between technology and erosion, and one must wonder where it will end. Problems are caused by the phenomenon known as 'peat shrinkage'. Peat is stable when in its natural, wet, condition; but once water is removed, the fibrous black peat changes colour to a reddish-brown, as it begins to oxidize. The process is known as humification: plant fibres lose their strength and the peat becomes light and fluffy; ploughing such land on windy days simply causes the humified peat to blow away. Several times our excavations at Fengate were covered with seed corn and granular fertilizer after a strong 'Fen blow'.

Peat 'shrinkage' is due to erosion and oxidation, and its effects can be devastating: at Flag Fen we have erected a post illustrating the various Fen surface levels and visitors can see that the modern ground level is the same as that in early Roman times; eighty years ago it would have been at least 2 m (6½ ft) higher. The process is seen to better effect in Holme Fen, in much deeper peat land. Here a cast-iron post reputedly (but improbably) removed

5 *Pollarded willows near Whittlesey, Cambs.*

6 *Pollarded willows being cut back in wintertime. It is essential to cut pollarded willows regularly if the trees are to remain healthy and vigorous.*

from the Crystal Palace site in 1852, was sunk through the peat and fixed onto oak piles which were in turn driven into the clay beneath, so that the top of the iron pillar was precisely level with the ground surface. Nearby Whittlesey Mere had just been drained, and although the land at Holme Fen was woodland, and not regularly ploughed, nevertheless the top of the post is now some 4 m (about $12\frac{1}{2}$ ft) above ground level (**3**). Peat wastage is to all intents and purposes irreversible: the 2 m ($6\frac{1}{2}$ ft) of peat lost at Flag Fen in the last eighty years would probably take two thousand to re-grow, provided that is, the land was allowed to revert to its original state.

In the eighteenth century, windmills, often in groups of six or ten or more, operated scoop wheels which lifted water from the dykes into the embanked rivers which flowed well above the level of the surrounding land. By the early nineteenth century the land surface continued to drop, as peat wastage maintained its inexorable process; soon windmills were barely able to cope. The introduction of the steam-engine just saved the hour: huge beam-engine pumps were installed to replace banks of windmills.

The new technology proved very effective and this was the period when the large Meres of Fenland, such as Soham and Whittlesey were drained. Soon more efficient steam pumps were required and these too began to feel the strain. In the twentieth century steam has been replaced by diesel and diesel in turn by submersible electric pumps. By now, however, there is relatively little peat left to shrink. Today most dykes are maintained almost dry, largely because it is cheaper to work this way. In Holland, on the other hand, drains are carefully kept full of water to prevent the peats from eroding away. In Fenland, trees and hedges are removed from dyke brinks to facilitate mechanical dredging which has to be carried out at regular intervals because dry or frozen soil soon blows in from the open land around. As dykes are cleaned out, they grow deeper and the land around becomes yet drier. So the vicious circle continues (**4**).

The undrained Fen was exploited in a variety of ways, which will be discussed in subsequent chapters, but they can be reduced to the bare essentials of life: fuel (wood and peat), food (fish, fowl and grazing) and shelter (reed and

7 *A dense growth of reed and sedge in a Fenland sedge bed; ideal thatching material.*

9 *The plastic 'skirt' around the edges of Flag Fen Mere.*

sedge thatch). The early drained Fen was also exploited in an 'environmentally friendly' way: geese and ducks were lured into decoys, willows were pollarded (**5** and **6**) for basket and hurdle osiers and sedge was grown in huge managed sedge beds (**7**).

'Bog oaks'

Perhaps the most dramatic illustration of the way drying-out is affecting the Fens is provided by 'bog oaks'. Fenland 'bog oaks' rarely come from bogs and are by no means always oaks; they are trees which have either been drowned when the Fen began to form and were subsequently preserved in the airless, waterlogged conditions, or else they are trees (often scots pine) which were growing in the fen deposits, during a dry spell. They catch on ploughs and can be very dangerous to the farmer. Some of the largest bog oaks – true oaks in this case – can be seen around the edges of fields that are on land once occupied by Whittlesey Mere and its surrounding fen. Some of the Whittlesey Mere bog oaks (**8**) are six thousand years old and the

8 *'Bog oaks' freshly removed from the ground near Ramsey Heights, Cambs. These oak trees were drowned by high ground-water levels about 6000 years ago.*

climatic record held in their growth-rings is of crucial importance.

I can remember driving around the lanes of the Holme Fen basin (where Whittlesey Mere once was) in the 1970s and seeing dozens of bog oaks being pulled from the ground. Today the 'harvest' is much poorer and yet another vitally important scientific resource is being sacrificed in favour of drainage. Today too there are strong rumours that the Holme Fen peats will be commercially mined for horticultural use. As I write I read in the *West Cambridgeshire Town Crier* that a new peat-cutting is to open in the Whittlesey Mere basin between Holme and Yaxley; they plan to extract 3000 tonnes of peat which 'is needed for horticulture'. The long-term effect on the local water-table could be disastrous. Is there no end to the extent we will abuse our surroundings?

Wetting the wetlands

Most informed opinion today would take a

10 *The model Bronze Age 'lake village' in the Flag Fen Mere, shortly after construction.*

balanced view of the drainage question, weighing the 'pros' of conservation against the 'cons' of agriculture. Just ten years ago, however, the cheap food argument would have prevailed absolutely: it was argued that one cannot have low cost, plentiful supplies of food and retain the traditional British countryside. Fenland soils are amongst the richest anywhere in Europe so, the argument went, it makes economic sense to drain them efficiently.

Today we realize that this policy has had, and is having, disastrous consequences on every aspect of the environment, but archaeology is seldom included in the reckoning. It is sometimes possible to repair damage to the natural environment (though many things such as small-scale species diversity are already damaged beyond recall). But archaeological sites are the product of our own species, and like the people who made them, each one is unique and irreplaceable; unfortunately these sites are being destroyed or damaged permanently.

The dilemma in the Fens is that drainage is revealing new sites, either through peat or soil

11 *The Flag Fen Mere planted with native British vegetation.*

erosion or by exposure in dykesides. Many hundreds of new sites have been discovered in the past ten years and most are suffering the ill-effects of drainage. So is it possible to re-wet them? The short answer is probably no. When a site has been pumped dry it is usually too late to do anything about it, other than a last-minute salvage excavation. Once peat begins to humify, the process is hard to arrest: it cracks and loses cohesion and the nutrient-rich (mainly nitrate) waters that percolate through it feed the newly-arrived micro-organisms. Indeed, once dried beyond a certain point, peat will actually repel water.

Sometimes one can anticipate events and take preventative action. In Somerset, for example, archaeologists working in close co-operation with the Nature Conservancy Council have preserved a length of the Neolithic Sweet Track (the world's oldest surviving trackway) in a nature reserve deep within the Levels. Sadly that is a rare success story.

In 1986 we realized that even the lowest-lying parts of Flag Fen were being adversely affected by drainage, so we approached the landowners, Anglian Water plc, in an attempt to do something about it. They very kindly leased us, at a peppercorn rent, the land we considered to be wettest, yet most at risk from drainage, and we set about building an artificial lake. The land around Flag Fen has been used for many years to provide settling-out beds for sewage sludge, and this is done by creating shallow basins within low soil banks, perhaps 1 m (3¼ ft) high. Sludge is then pumped in and after a few months the water evaporates and the land can be ploughed and sowed.

We had observed this process for some time and decided to try a variant of it ourselves. A machine was hired, and a low, but substantial bank was erected around the area we wanted to flood. The next step was to borrow an enormous pump from Anglian Water and to start pumping from the nearby dyke. The embanked 'lagoon' began to fill quite rapidly; at the time, I reckoned it would require at least ten hours to fill completely, so I went home for the night. Next morning I arrived at Flag Fen and to my surprise saw that the lagoon was no wetter than I had left it on the previous afternoon; if anything it was slightly drier. I then visited the archaeological excavation and was horrified to see water literally squirting from cracks in the trench sides into the excavation: a few posts protruded above the turbulent waters, much as they might have done in the Bronze Age. The farmer's field next door was looking distinctly damp and the normally dry dyke between it and our land was full. The operation had been an unqualified disaster.

We waited for three days for the waters to subside and I took advice from John Green, a long-time Fen farmer. We had discussed the possibility that the peats would be too cracked and dry to retain water sometime previously, and he had suggested that we insert a polythene film through the earth bank and press it into the clay below the peat, some 3 m (10 ft) down.

It sounded a straightforward operation, but in the event it was fraught with problems, as we did not have time to let the ground dry out fully after our first attempt at flooding. The summer of 1987 was also one of the wettest on record, and I have grim memories of battling with wet, peaty, sludgy plastic (9).

Four days later, we had buried some 400 m (1320 ft) of thick builder's polythene and were ready to resume pumping. This time the banks and the plastic film below held. After three days the lake was full and the model of the Bronze Age island that we had built in the dry, on the off-chance that the lake would eventually flood, suddenly seemed less ridiculous (10). Just seven days after inserting the plastic membrane, Lord Montagu of Beaulieu, Chairman of English Heritage, opened our Visitor Centre to the public. It had been a rather anxious week.

We originally intended to use the lake to keep a large part of Flag Fen wet for future excavation, but now we would like to see whether longer term preservation might be possible. Already wildlife is colonizing the water and its fringes, sometimes with some help from us: we have planted hundreds of willows, alder and reeds, and, of course the flower after which Flag Fen was named: the native British yellow flag iris, *Iris pseudacorus*. Three years after making the lake, we have large populations of reed buntings, wrens, wagtails, moorhens, geese and duck. Late one summer I saw two kingfishers emerge from a hole in the bank on the far side of the lake, and I have seen them a few times subsequently. It was planned to open that side of the lake as a public walkway, but the birds must take preference. In its small way, the lake at Flag Fen illustrates that archaeology and nature conservation cannot be separated (11).

2

Archaeology in the Peterborough area

Before the archaeological story proper can begin it is necessary to discuss the techniques which we used to find the sites, and then to excavate them; the delicate topics of funding and display will also be mentioned at the end of the chapter. Deeply buried sites were found by a procedure we largely invented ourselves and have since termed 'dyke survey', but material nearer the surface was revealed by the more conventional technique of aerial photography – a method of prospection that has been extensively used by archaeologists since the First World War.

Cropmarks and aerial photographs

The archaeological importance of the Peterborough fen-edge was first revealed by chance discoveries during gravel-digging. Aerial photographs taken after the Second World War, however, showed that the small pre-war gravel pits had only just nibbled at a tiny part of a large ancient landscape. Huge areas of Fengate could be seen to be covered with a mass of long-lost ditches, pits, wells and other signs of human activity. All these archaeological features were entirely buried and no trace of them survived on the surface; their presence was revealed only by uneven crop growth which, when viewed from the air, could be seen to form coherent patterns which were plainly man-made. These differences of crop growth form patterns known as 'cropmarks'.

The principle of cropmark formation is quite straightforward: when a ditch or hole is dug it usually becomes filled-in by natural weathering and ploughing and the ground is levelled so that nothing is visible on the surface. Deeply buried, the ditch or hole has usually been filled in with water-retentive ancient topsoil which

the roots of plants growing on the modern surface seek out in preference to the undisturbed subsoil around it. So plants growing directly above these deep, moist ancient features grow faster and more lushly, and they also mature earlier. By the same token, plants growing above buried stone walls, or paved roads, grow feebly; this impoverished growth shows up from the air as a pale or 'negative cropmark'. The best example of a negative cropmark at Fengate is the parch-mark in permanent pasture left by the Fen Causeway Roman Road (**12** and **13**).

Experience has shown that cropmarks are most pronounced in years with a dry growing season, such as 1976 or 1989. Cereal crops usually display the best marks, but sugarbeet and rape can also be quite good; potatoes and old pasture, on the other hand, are almost useless. The nature of the ground below the topsoil (the subsoil) can also affect cropmark formation: poorly draining subsoils like clay show virtually nothing, but freely-draining sand and gravel land is excellent; chalk and limestone can be very good too. In the deep Fens the interpretation of cropmarks can be complicated by the existence of the ancient filled-in tidal creeks or roddons (**14**).

The subsoil of most of Fengate is freely-draining river gravel which was laid down during and shortly after the Ice Age. Lower-lying parts of the site are cloaked in fen deposits, such as peat and river-borne clay (alluvium); these effectively mask and then bury the gravels, so that land below about 3 m (9½ ft) above modern sea level (Ordnance Datum is its technical name) simply does not show cropmarks. In these low-lying, deeply buried areas around the edges of Flag Fen, aerial photogra-

25

12 *The main area of cropmarks at Fengate. (Cambridge University Collection: copyright reserved.)*

phy does not work, and we have to use other techniques such as 'dyke survey' to reveal the ancient landscape.

Techniques of excavation
The popular image of an archaeological dig is of deep, narrow, unshored trenches with local workmen carrying baskets filled with soil on their heads, whilst others scrabble around on their hands and knees wielding anything from a pick and shovel to a fine-haired paintbrush or pointing trowel. However, in lowland Britain such small 'keyhole' trenches, as they are known, are of very little use if one wishes to understand how a settlement or landscape developed. So to meet the challenges of expos-

ing huge or 'open areas' to scrutiny, British archaeologists developed a number of techniques. General Pitt-Rivers, the father of modern excavation, worked a system of advancing trenches, whereby his workmen dumped the spoil from a new area on the one that had just been completed, and so on. The problem with this system was that although a large area might eventually be exposed, it was only actually visible in long, thin strips; it was impossible ever to see a decent-sized area open at any one time. Subsequent re-excavation has shown that this system caused even the great General to miss many important observations.

It was not really until the Second World War that it became possible to clear large areas of land at any one time, by using powerful earthmoving machines. In Britain Professor W.F. Grimes had the task of examining bomber airfields before the runways were laid, and he sometimes used towed scrapers to remove the topsoil before excavation. London's Heathrow airport was one wartime base excavated by Professor Grimes and few passengers there can know that their jumbo jets land and take off on the site of a highly important Romano-Celtic temple.

There is no doubt that if it had not been for earthmoving machines, neither Fengate nor Flag Fen could have been properly discovered or excavated. I have written about archaeological earthmoving elsewhere and this is not the place for a technical discussion, but basically we use two types of machine. First a bulk

13 *Explanation of cropmarks visible in (12): (A) Bronze Age field and drove boundary ditches; (B) Fen Causeway Roman road; (C) Cat's Water Roman farmyards; (D) Late Neolithic ring-ditch. (Martin Redding.)*

earthmover removes soil that lies a safe distance above the sensitive archaeological levels; these, however, are heavy machines that can only be used on deeply buried sites (**15 and 16**). Next, when about 15 cm (6 in.) above archaeologically important layers, we employ a digger with a broad and toothless bucket to remove the remaining soil with great delicacy and precision. Diggers can either be of the familiar tractor-style, usually for smaller trenches, or the rotating, tracked sort. A good operator should be able to lift an egg intact if he is in proper control of his machine. I have seen students do more damage to archaeological features with a small pointing trowel than a good driver with a powerful hydraulic digger.

The surface of the topsoil is carefully searched and metal-detected before the machines move in. The topsoil and overburden is then removed. The next stage is to place a

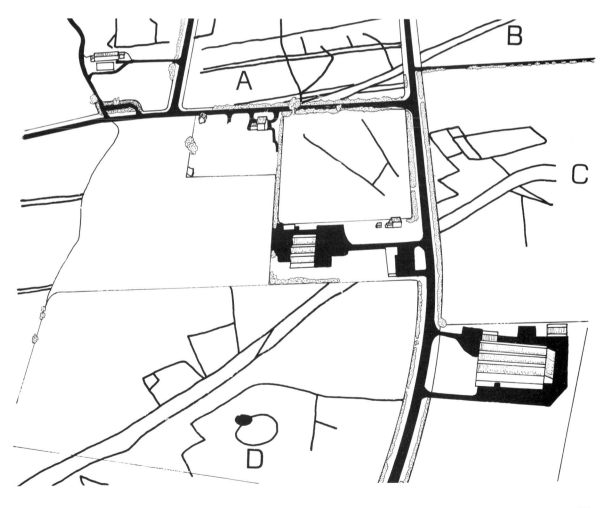

grid of posts – usually 10 m (33 ft) apart – across the stripped area. These posts form the essential framework upon which everything subsequently depends: anything excavated is mapped, plotted and planned by reference to the site grid. It should be as accurate as possible, but in my experience it often seems jinxed. I will give two examples.

I directed the Fengate excavations while employed full-time in Canada at the Royal Ontario Museum. This meant that I was in Peterborough during the digging season (April–October), but as soon as the dig closed I returned to Toronto. Frequently we would excavate in the same area from one season to

14 *Aerial view of bare earth fields in central Fenland, showing the tree-like network of prehistoric 'roddons' or tidal creeks. (Cambridge University Collection: copyright reserved.)*

15 *Bulk earthmoving, Fengate 1972: a self-powered scraper.*

another and it was essential that the site grids married-up from one year to the next, with absolute precision. During my first absence from England during the winter of 1971/72 we left our trenches open, complete with grid pegs in neat squares, only to return the following spring to find they had all been used to fuel gypsy fires. Not one peg survived! The next winter I was determined not to allow a repetition of this, so I carefully placed a row of pegs within the roots of a large thorn hedge and then concreted them in place – gilding the lily one might suppose, but no: the next spring (1973) I returned to find that a new sewer had been placed along the line of the hedge which had been completely removed – along with my grid.

While site grids could cause problems, the weather of south-east Britain frequently caused more: the summer of 1961 was at times appalling, and our elderly visitors were put in mind of the trenches of the Somme (17); towards the end of most summers mists would drift in from the deeper Fen and communication around the site could become distinctly hazardous. In conditions like these, textbooks are useless and one muddles through, in the fond hope that it will turn out right some day – as it usually does.

It is necessary here to say a few words about how the excavation of Fengate – the area of Peterborough we had been assigned to investigate ahead of development – was organized. Today virtually the whole suburb is built-over, but when we started work in 1971 there were farms, fields and hedges. Many of the trenches opened-up were actually excavated simultaneously and we decided it would be less chaotic if certain key areas could be treated as entirely separate projects, with their own series of finds' numbers, plans, maps and notes; although notionally separate, all were done to the same standards, using the same conventions and criteria.

So Fengate was divided into sub-sites, each one of which had several trenches, which are shown on the map (18) in solid black. Vicarage Farm, Padholme Road, Newark Road, Storey's Bar Way, Cat's Water and Fourth Drove were excavated between 1971 and 1978; Power Station in 1989. Flag Fen notionally starts at the Cat's Water drain, which marks the modern boundary between dryland and wetland, but it is in fact part of the Fengate landscape, only more deeply buried and wetter.

The Fengate sub-sites were excavated using open-area techniques; after mechanical removal of the overburden the gravel surface would be scraped clean using ordinary garden onion-hoes (19). This was very tiring but it was quick and effective – certainly far better than trowelling on hands and knees. The effect of hoeing was to remove any loose soil that might obscure the gravel surface below. When freshly hoed clean the gravel had a strange mottled

orange, brown and grey appearance; in part the mottled effect was caused by permafrost during and just after the last Ice Age, and the skill was to distinguish these purely natural effects from those left by the hand of man. It was often very difficult and I have frequently spent time and money meticulously excavating the remains of Ice Age frost cracks and ice-wedges.

Man-made disturbances of the gravel subsoil usually have a coherence and pattern that makes them obvious when seen over a large area that has been freshly hoed(20); but when viewed in a keyhole trench they are very nearly impossible to distinguish from Ice Age marks. On the whole, man-made disturbances are quite dark and usually have crisp edges. Large archaeological (as opposed to geological) features thus exposed are then rapidly mapped and areas to be excavated are marked out with string, so that when heavy rain or prolonged sunshine eventually obliterate the hoed surface we do not have to re-hoe.

Generally speaking large archaeological features, such as field boundary or drainage ditches, are only sample-excavated – it simply

16 The huge area of Fengate exposed required three successive types of machinery: first the bulk scraping (15), this was followed by a tracked loader and at least one wheeled-digger.

17 *Fengate after heavy rain.*

would not be cost-effective to empty them in their entirety. This accounts for the unexcavated 'baulks' (which look like neat soil walls) that have been left at regular intervals across ditches and other linear features, such as house foundations (see **34**). The baulks allow us to examine how a ditch filled in – was it by natural (weathering) processes or was it back-filled by man? We can also see evidence in the baulks for redigging and in certain cases the dry surface can be used to take solid block-like samples for subsequent microscopic examination in the laboratory. Every archaeologist knows that you can judge the quality of an excavation by the longevity of its baulks: wobbly-sided baulks soon get wet and collapse. Some of the Cat's Water sub-site baulks were still standing three years after their excavation. I shall say no more.

Inevitably the popular imagination is caught by the process of actual excavation: revealing the buried past by removing soil; but what few people realize is that more time is spent on most excavations mapping what is in the ground (**21**) and recording finds on endless lists. Every scrap of pottery, for example, must be given a unique number, grid reference, layer number, level (usually in metres above sea level) and brief description. This information is listed (**22**) and marked onto the find's individual bag.

'Open area' techniques cannot be applied to most waterlogged sites, unless one has limitless sources of manpower and money. So Flag Fen, unlike sites in Fengate, was, and is, being excavated using 'keyhole' trenches. To give an idea of the problems we face, our current main excavation at Flag Fen measures a mere 7 x 9 m (22 x 30 ft), yet it has produced nearly 20,000 pieces of wood and timber – and each one has to be planned, recorded, lifted, sampled and catalogued. In 1989 it took as much manpower to excavate the keyhole at Flag Fen as the huge open area (roughly 200 m (2153 ft) square) at the Power Station sub-site.

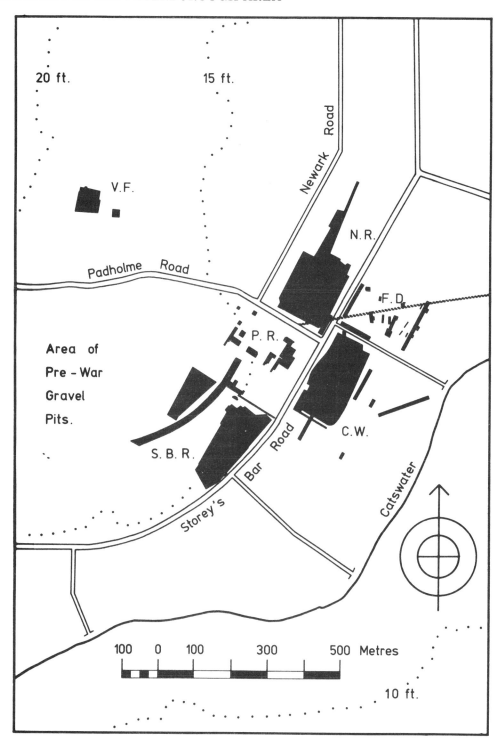

18 *Map of Fengate showing the location of various sub-sites of the campaign of the 1971–78:*
VF Vicarage Farm; PR Padholme Road; NR *Newark Road; SBW Storey's Bar Way; CW Cat's Water; FD Fourth Drove. Trenches are shown in black, the Roman road is shown by a slashed line. (Robert Powell.)*

19 *Onion hoes being used for the final cleaning of the surface first exposed by the self-powered scraper (Fengate 1972).*

Excavation techniques at Flag Fen are rather special and will be discussed further in chapter 4; the main problem to note, however, is that ancient wood loses most of its 'woodiness', which has been replaced by minerals and water so it must be kept wet at all times – even when one is not actually digging. This causes the most horrendous practical problems, since failure to keep the site moist is accompanied by irreversible damage; unhappily dry ancient wood cannot be restored to its former state. Once dried-out, no amount of water can close the splits and cracks that then appear.

The early years at Flag Fen were largely spent inventing new techniques of excavation; for example, hand-watering via watering cans was replaced in 1985 by a splendid, if somewhat ancient, agricultural sprinkling system powered by a friend's venerable Ferguson tractor (see **66**). The trouble was that the water supply came from a dyke, and every time we sprinkled the site we liberally peppered it with the seeds and pollen of the aquatic plants growing in the dyke. This caused our (palaeo-) botanist much grief, as he was not used to seeing his supposedly ancient samples sprout like so much mustard and cress; now we keep the site wet using the town mains, and reflect that we live in a topsy-turvy world where the Fens have to be sprinkled with water from an upland reservoir 32 km (20 miles) away.

Finally a word about the concept 'site'. This is a catch-all word beloved of archaeologists. Sometimes it is used to refer to anything at hand, as in 'Please do not drop cigarette-ends on the site'. Sometimes it refers to a modern area of land: thus Fengate is a site; Flag Fen is a site. Most commonly it is used to describe what archaeologists still sometimes call a 'field monument' where 'monument' means anything old above or below the ground. Each individual example counts as a site, and this use of the word causes problems at Fengate and other regions that were continuously and densely occupied in the past.

What are the sites, as in 'field monuments', of Fengate and Flag Fen? One or two are obvious: the Flag Fen timber platform (chapter 5) or the Site 11 ditched enclosure (chapter 3). But what about the huge Fengate ditched fields and droveways? Are these a site, and if so, where are its edges? It is just this sort of problem that has led archaeologists to move away from the 'site' concept and replace it with the less specific idea of 'landscape'. At Fengate and Flag Fen, then, we are examining parts of a superbly preserved ancient landscape – with 'sites' on it, it is true – but the whole is far more important than the sum of its individual parts.

The new 'landscape' way of looking at the past makes good philosophical sense, as it stresses the integration of people with their surroundings. It also accords well with current 'Green' thinking which emphasizes the unity of man and nature. Sadly archaeological legislation still protects individual, specified Scheduled Monuments, rather than whole stretches

of countryside; this must change.

Landscapes – old and new
Peterborough, or Medeshamstede to give it its medieval name, has always been a prosperous place; indeed its other, unofficial, medieval name was Guildenburg – or city of gold. The riches derived ultimately from the city's location at the edge of two worlds, one wet, one dry. There have, of course, been disadvantages to this prime location: it was plundered by the legendary Hereward the Wake and more recently the Victorian railway barons destroyed most of its Georgian and medieval buildings in their confident 'improvements'. Modern developments have not always been completely successful; to see good Fenland townscapes, go to Spalding or Wisbech, two of the least spoilt towns in England.

The city's Saxon past is less clearly understood, but the church that was ultimately to become the magnificent cathedral of St Peter, has its origins in this period. The region has a very illustrious Roman past with a substantial 'half-legionary' fortress within the city limits at

20 *Unexcavated ditches showing up as dark soil-filled marks on the surface (Fengate 1978).*

21 *Planning Bronze Age ditches to achieve a rapid, but accurate plan of the excavations.*

Longthorpe. Just to the west lies the prosperous Roman market town of *Durobrivae* (modern Water Newton), on Ermine Street (today the A1 or Great North Road), the find-spot of the magnificent Water Newton treasure – the earliest church plate from northern Europe, now on display in the British Museum. Outside the walled town, in its *vicus*, or suburbs, were the workshops of the potters who made Nene Valley ware, one of the most frequently found types of British-made Roman pottery. Slightly set back from the smut and grime of industry, and in commanding locations overlooking the Nene Valley were the villas of the well-off.

In pre-Roman times the Peterborough region was prosperous, but perhaps less oppressively so than in Roman times. The main area known to us of this period is Fengate and we assume – for there are no written records to tell us so – that this part of eastern Peterborough was selected because it lay immediately next to the watery Fen. Based at Fengate, prehistoric communities most certainly had the best of both the worlds that Hugh Candidus wrote about in the extract quoted at the very beginning of this book. In winter they had access to almost limitless supplies of fish, eels and wildfowl; while elsewhere in lowland England people scraped around to find winter protein, in Fengate it was in abundant supply. In the late spring the lush meadows of the Fen edge could be cut for hay and the wetland pastures could survive in even the hottest, driest of summers. In the autumn there were reeds for thatching and peat could be cut at any time of the year. There is also good evidence to suggest

Welland Valley Project Finds Sheet (25/6/80)   Top

Tick for Computer :   Site Code :

Finds Plan   Add 2 Grid Points & Labelled Section Lines.

If Not Planned Here State Where.

METHOD (M): Fengate Shovel = F ; Wet Sieve = WS ; Dry Sieve = DS ; Other = O [Use Notes]

No.	Lr.	East	West	Dpth	Type	M	Box	No.	Lr.	East	West	Dpth	Type	M	Box

Welland Valley Project Finds Sheet (25/6/80)   Top

Notes : [brief description of feature, etc]

| Structure : | Feature : | Section : | to |
| Date Dug : | Dug By : | Page | of |

22 *Printed finds sheets were first used at Fengate in 1973. Each list would include a sketch-plan of the relevant part of the site.*

that salt, always a very valuable commodity, was extracted from saline water simply by heating it up in shallow trays.

While the Fens provided a wealth of natural resources the flood-free (roughly speaking any ground today above the 4 m (12½ ft) contour line) land of Fengate and Peterborough provided a safe haven for people or livestock in the wet months. It is freely-draining gravel land, ideally suited for the growing of crops such as wheat and barley. Given such a diverse and rich environment it is surely little wonder that the area was so heavily and continuously settled from earliest times.

The edge of the Fen would have crept westwards as the general level of fen flooding rose. We have seen that this started on lower-lying, mainly river valley land, towards the Wash, but the higher, landward edges of the Fen basin took longer to become waterlogged. At Fengate we suspect, but cannot yet prove

beyond all doubt, that Flag Fen and the land around it was becoming distinctly damp at sometime around 2000 BC. By about 1500 BC, conditions were probably wet enough to allow wood to become permanently waterlogged, and thus preserved for posterity; viewed in a wider, Fenland, perspective this is late in the story of Fen formation. Certainly by 1000 BC Flag Fen was under shallow water which lapped up against dry land at Fengate perhaps 200 m (660 ft) north and west of the Cat's Water, the artificial drain that notionally separates Fengate (dryland) from Flag Fen (wetland).

The Cat's Water drain itself poses an archaeological problem. The generally accepted view is that it was dug in post-Roman times, perhaps as early as the sixth century AD; no one can be certain of its function, but it might have acted as a 'catchwater' that prevented water from the higher land of the Fen margins from inundating the Fen proper. Its curving, twisting path suggests that in places, like Fengate, it might have followed a natural course, but we cannot be certain; elsewhere it is undoubtedly entirely man-made.

The Cat's Water marks a convenient boundary between prehistoric Fen and dryland. To the north-west the gravel subsoil gently rises until it reaches 5 or 6 m (16 or 19 ft) above sea level – well beyond the danger of seasonal flooding. This is where the old, original Peterborough is located; after about 1970, factory development has crept south-east, up to the very edge of the Cat's Water, a mere 2 m (6½ ft) or so, above sea level.

The topsoil of Fengate west of the Cat's Water is heavily bound with river-borne (alluvial) clays. These were mostly deposited in Roman times and are thickest where the land drops away, towards the Cat's Water. Alluvial clay was almost absent on the Vicarage Farm sub-site, thicker at Padholme Road and Newark Road and almost 1 m (3¼ ft) thick on lower-lying parts of the Cat's Water and Power Station sub-sites.

On the fenward, south-east, side of the Cat's Water the gravel and clay subsoil gently dips so that it is almost 1 m (3¼ ft) below sea level underneath the Flag Fen artificial lake. Above it is a buried and sodden ancient topsoil, a layer of peat of varying thickness that accumulated in the Bronze Age and above that a thick deposit of peaty clay alluvium. There are hints that this last deposit was not entirely river-borne when first laid down; some micro-organisms found in it are the type that can tolerate brackish, or semi-salt water conditions. Today the River Nene is tidal at the Dog-in-a-Doublet sluice, just 5 km (3 miles) due east of Flag Fen.

The superficially flat countryside is in fact very complex and conceals within its buried layers evidence for an evolving landscape of people, plants and animals. The complexities of this story have been slowly and hesitantly unravelled by generations of antiquarians, geologists and archaeologists; unfortunately there is only space here to summarize the most significant advances, but the story is continuing, and while there is research there is hope.

Pioneers in Peterborough
The Peterborough region has a distinguished history of archaeological research. If we set aside such a coincidence as the birth of William Stukeley (arguably the most distinguished antiquarian of all) in Stamford, just outside the limits of the modern city, and concentrate on those who were active in the region, the cast is indeed extraordinary. First and foremost,

although not concerned with pre-Roman archaeology, was Lord Fitzwilliams' agent E.T. Artis. Artis was working in the mid-nineteenth century with the flair and bravura of the best Victorians. He is reckoned by many to be Britain's first serious rescue archaeologist and provides a good example to many today in that he wrote up his work. I personally admire the way he removed a Roman mosaic to the floor of his master's dairy at Milton Hall, where it can now be admired by a select few on the very outskirts of Peterborough.

Artis knew the 'peasant poet' John Clare who came from Helpston, just north of Peterborough. Both of them witnessed the construction of the Great Northern railway through the flat fenny country around Helpston, on its way from King's Cross, ultimately to Edinburgh. Clare's memorial in Helpston churchyard, 'A Poet is Born not Made' ought equally to apply to archaeologists.

The story of pre-Roman research really begins with George Wyman Abbott. Abbott was a successful solicitor in Peterborough and indeed the firm of Wyman and Abbott (George united the two families by marriage) still prospers to this day. As a very young man he would visit the hand-worked gravel pits of Fengate and collect antiquities from the workmen. He kept notebooks that were as detailed as could be expected under the circumstances and have subsequently proved very useful. Abbott knew the leading archaeologists of the day and in 1910 published the first account of his work in collaboration with the distinguished Neolithic specialist, Reginald Smith.

The Abbott and Smith paper of 1910 described a type of highly-decorated and often crudely-made, thick-walled Neolithic pottery as being in the Peterborough tradition. The term is in common use today. Their seminal paper was followed in 1922 by the work of the equally distinguished archaeologist E.T. Leeds, whose family comes from Eye, a small village just east of Peterborough. Leeds published more of Abbott's pottery finds, but this time mainly of the earlier Bronze Age, Beaker style. Again, it was a paper that had a considerable influence.

Leeds and Smith might have been a difficult act to follow, but in 1945 Clare I. Fell published the results of her investigations of Abbott's Iron Age finds, together with Christopher Hawkes. This paper, despite the difficult times (1945), also made an immediate and profound impression, and Barry Cunliffe was later to use the name Fengate/Cromer to describe an Early Iron Age pottery 'style zone'.

By now the Fengate archaeological pantheon was distinctly top-heavy, but more was to come: in 1956 Dr Isobel Smith wrote the most quoted unpublished reference in British archaeology: her doctoral thesis at the Institute of Archaeology, University of London. This outstanding piece of scholarship placed British Neolithic pottery studies on sure foundations; she used previously unillustrated late Neolithic pottery from Abbott's Fengate collection to exemplify 'Fengate ware'. Fengate ware is a very diagnostic style of late Neolithic pottery that has many stylistic traits in common with important Early Bronze Age pottery styles, such as Collared Urns (named because of their exaggerated and thickened rims). So what with 'the Peterborough tradition', 'Fengate ware' and the 'Fengate/Cromer style-zone', all names of important Neolithic, Bronze and Iron Age pottery styles, the region has made a very considerable mark on the development of British prehistoric scholarship.

Despite their writings, none of the important scholars just mentioned lifted so much as a piece of turf of Fengate soil, although Leeds excavated some barrows at Eyebury, 3.2 km (2 miles) away, just before the First World War; all relied on Abbott, and he did not let them down. His contribution to British prehistory is, therefore, profound.

Abbott and his collaborators had placed Peterborough firmly on the archaeological map. The next important development was in the late 1960s, when central government decided to make Peterborough the site of a New Town – one of an outer ring, designed to take London's 'overspill' population. In 1968 the Nene Valley Research Committee, a group of local people and archaeologists interested in the area, commissioned the Royal Commission on Historical Monuments to undertake a survey of the antiquities threatened by the proposed New Town. Christopher Taylor carried out the archaeological research for the Commission and his results were published in 1968. This report: *Peterborough New Town: a Survey of the Antiquities in the Areas of Development* was the first thorough attempt to relate Fengate finds to the Peterborough landscape. The task was not at all straightforward: the small gravel pits visited by Abbott changed hands regularly and their owners were not concerned about quarrying-out one area before starting another. Although he made sterling efforts to sort out the muddle, Christopher Taylor warned me from the outset not to take pre-war findspots too literally; all that we can be reasonably certain of is that most finds came from Fengate – indeed, that is all we need to know in most cases.

The Royal Commission 'Peterborough Volume' (as it is known for short) published the first detailed aerial photographs of Fengate and other sites around the city. These were mainly taken by Professor J.K. St Joseph of Cambridge University, a pioneer in the field and perhaps the finest-ever exponent of the art; they were outstanding.

The year 1968 also saw the first post-war excavation at Fengate, at a spot named Site 11, after its number in the Peterborough Volume. This dig was directed by Christine Mahany for the Nene Valley Research Committee; I was able to write the report on this very unusual site recently and it will be discussed in the next chapter.

At this point in the story I must introduce myself: while working for Dr Doug Tushingham at the Royal Ontario Museum, Toronto, I found myself in England with instructions to see whether it would be possible for the Museum to mount a dig there. I had no idea where to go, but had read an article in the excellent journal *Current Archaeology*, just before I boarded the plane; in it, the editor, Andrew Selkirk, had reviewed the 'Peterborough Volume' and had even suggested that the threat to such an important area was so serious that the Americans might be called in. It was a long shot, and Canadians are most decidedly not Americans, but it set my mind working.

So in the summer of 1971 I found myself working as a site supervisor for Dr John Peter Wild at Longthorpe, now part of the western New Town, and following this I was able to negotiate a deal whereby I was to return from Canada the following year and direct excavations at Fengate, on behalf of the Royal Ontario Museum and the Nene Valley Research Committee. Thus started eight years of jet-lag and transatlantic commuting: summers in England, winters in Canada. The then Chairman of the Nene Valley Research Committee was the pioneer of open-area excavation, Professor W.F. Grimes who had directed wartime airfield excavations. So when it became quite apparent that Fengate could only be tackled using open-area techniques, I had a firm ally in high places.

I will never forget Professor Grimes' first inspection of our work. Two days before his official arrival I had everyone make the site spotless; not a pebble was out of place. I had to collect him from the station, so I did not report to site first thing in the morning. My ancient Land Rover pulled out of the station car-park and we drove through Peterborough the long way so that my nerves could settle down. When we arrived on site a humorist had placed inverted-bucket sand-castles, hundreds of them, along the crest of every spoil heap and on either side of the trackway leading to the site hut. Professor Grimes, to his eternal credit, pretended not to notice, but it took a good while to restore my sense of humour.

The Fengate project started in 1971 and ran until 1978, and is published in four monographs, the last of which appeared in 1984. Our team then turned its attentions to the north side of Peterborough, in the lower Welland valley. We mainly worked on Neolithic sites near the archaeologically well-known village of Maxey which sits on a large gravel island surrounded by a seasonally-flooded river floodplain. The excavations of 1979–82 have recently been published.

In 1979 I was invited on a lecture tour of the Netherlands and while I was there I met a number of Dutch colleagues who were working in very Fen-like surroundings. They discovered new sites by searching through material that had been dredged from drainage ditches (Dutch dykes unlike ours are banks). In Holland they keep their ditches full of water to prevent peat erosion, but it struck me that we could do something similar in Fenland, but instead of searching the up-cast on the edge of ditches, we could actually look at the dry ditch sides themselves. We called this technique 'dyke survey' and found it a very effective and low-cost means of discovering sites deeply buried beneath fen peats, silts and other water-borne deposits.

I put forward a scheme for a small-scale dyke survey in the Peterborough region to English Heritage who, to my surprise, decided to fund it. I was delighted at this far-sighted decision, as I knew full well that many people in establishment circles were highly sceptical of our ideas. That was how in November 1982 I happened to find myself walking along a dyke just to the east of Fengate. I stumbled across a piece of oak lying in the mud, slid down the dykeside almost to the water, scraped around in the ooze – and came up with more oak wood. That wood came from the foundations of the Flag Fen Late Bronze Age timber platform, to be discussed in Chapter 5.

Funding and display

When I started work in Fengate, the total annual budget for the 1971 season was about £3000, of which at least half was spent on earthmoving. Today Flag Fen costs English Heritage some £80,000 per annum in grants; even so, it is quite inexpensive: an equivalent urban excavation might easily cost upward of half a million pounds.

It is often said that the excavation of a wetland site costs ten times more than its equivalent on dry land. This is because wetland excavation is very slow and painstaking, and involves the taking of numerous samples for botanists and other specialists. We could easily double our current Flag Fen budget, but the additional progress made would be, I suspect, negligible, as it would take much internal reorganization to convert from a fairly small operation to a major project. A good archaeologist tries to see at what point he or she is starting to waste money, as there is a limit beyond which increased funding becomes almost self-defeating. It is as if each project has an internal governor which dictates the scale appropriate to the operation.

The figure I mentioned for Flag Fen includes what is known as post-excavation research – the writing of scholarly reports and books such as this. Some archaeologists feel that post-excavation costs should be many times greater than the actual cost of excavation. Others, such as myself, feel that this is not necessary: we should only remove from the ground what we can hope to process within a reasonable time, and at reasonable cost. Otherwise we should leave well alone – even if destruction is inevitable.

Post-excavation research at Flag Fen mainly takes place in the winter, although tree-ring studies and certain other woody researches that cannot wait, continue throughout the year. Our method is fairly simple: we dig little and often, and try to keep on top of the publication and research 'backlog'; if this gets too huge we pull people in from the dig and have them help the post-excavation effort.

The Department of the Environment Inspectorate of Ancient Monuments, before they became English Heritage, funded most of the Fengate project, the entire dyke survey and Flag Fen. Taken together this grant-support must have amounted to over £1 million since 1971. Flag Fen will have received £475,000 when English Heritage withdraws grant-aid in April 1992. By then they will have been funding the project for a decade and it is reasonable to suggest that we should find our future funds elsewhere; Flag Fen is being funded from English Heritage's rescue archaeology budget and other sites threatened with destruction will suffer if we at Flag Fen do nothing to achieve a measure of self-support. Flag Fen is, as we shall see, under serious threat of destruction through drying-out, but it is essentially a long-term threat and not like the instant obliteration posed by a gravel pit or motorway.

So 1 April 1992 will be a crucial day. Thereafter Flag Fen must support itself through income raised by visitors' entrance money. We need some 50,000 visitors to have any hope of survival: in 1989 we attracted almost 16,000; so there is some way yet to go! Flag Fen is run by Fenland Archaeological Trust, a non-profit-making limited company with charitable status; all money taken at the door or from secondary sales must be devoted to Fenland archaeological research. The Trust publishes a regular Newsletter and has an active Friends organization. We try to involve schools in our work at Flag Fen, both in helping outdoors, and by communicating with the post-excavation team via our computers which are linked to the educational electronic mail network. We are the only continuing excavation with direct links to the classroom – and tomorrow's archaeologists.

3

The first farmers (4000-2000 BC)

Introduction: putting sites in their setting
One of the great pleasures of archaeology is that it never stands still. Ideas are constantly evolving; old concepts are replaced by new ones; then a few years later the old views are re-accepted, in a modified form – only to be thrown out again, when the next generation stamps its mark on the subject – and so the process continues. Thirty years ago archaeologists viewed the British Neolithic largely from a Wessex perspective; I suspect because that was the area with the huge monuments and the great collective tombs. It was also the area where the antiquarians and archaeologists of the past three hundred years often did their most important work: what happened in the Avebury or Stonehenge region set the pattern for elsewhere. The two decades on either side of the Second World War were a time when archaeologists explained many phenomena they did not fully understand by invoking 'diffusion' or 'influence' from outside.

For instance, once farmers or farming had arrived in Britain, subsequent new ideas, especially the earliest types of metalwork were then thought to have diffused outwards from a supposed Wessex heartland into the less favoured regions of Britain. Indeed, by the earliest Bronze Age, say 2000 BC, the process seemed to have become so well-established, that archaeologists were able to talk of a 'Wessex Culture' which was seen to have a very strong 'influence' on the surrounding country.

Today, British archaeologists tend to be more pragmatic and would only accept a given region's primacy, if it could be demonstrated – for example by independent evidence, such as radiocarbon dating. It is then necessary to seek a reason for these phenomena – what was the wealth, for example, actually based upon? This healthy scepticism has had a liberating effect on the regions of Britain: for example, the numerous holes or pits dug into the gravel sub-soil of Fengate by prehistoric people were once interpreted by scholars in what one might term 'the Wessex manner'. On dry chalkland such pits might well have been dug to store grain; on the other hand, on the fen-edge even the shallowest hole will swiftly fill with water as the winter ground-water-table rises, and any grain within it would rapidly revert to an evil-smelling sludge. Wells on the chalk may have to penetrate great depths; for example the Bronze Age Wilsford Shaft, was cut through the Wiltshire chalk an astonishing 33 m (100 ft). On the fen-edge, however, most wells reach to the 'sock', or water-table, rarely deeper than a man's waist. So a well in Fengate would be a storage pit in Wessex. It seems obvious now, but thirty and forty years ago Wyman Abbott's Fengate wells were all interpreted as storage pits or silos. In the chalkland, prehistoric pits dug about 1 m (3¼ ft) deep were filled with grain and capped-off. The grain around the outside would act as a type of buffer-zone that protected the bulk of the deposit from destruction. Such a system would not work in waterlogged or poorly drained sub-soils, such as Fengate.

Misinterpreting a single type of feature might not seem very important, but in reality it was: material accumulates slowly in a well, as people throw items in, one-by-one, perhaps for luck. This means that pottery and other things found together there might easily have been accumulating over several centuries, obviously depending upon the use-life of the well itself. However, to explain this as a short-lived, or rapidly accumulated 'closed' group of finds could be very archaeologically misleading, since the so-called 'closed group' is neither closed nor are the items in it contemporary. Furthermore, the idea of a large storage pit presupposes a permanently settled group of people to guard it; it also assumes large quantities of grain. We will see in the following chapters that neither can be assumed for Fengate; indeed, the contrary was probably the case.

The main point to arise from this discussion is that archaeological 'features', in other words the basic building-bricks that we use to form our interpretations of ancient sites (items such as ditches, gullies, wells, scoops, pits and post-holes) may well be common to most areas of Britain, but they can and must be interpreted in different ways, depending on each individual site's physical surroundings and the prevailing ancient social and environmental context. The former are fairly straightforward to reconstruct, providing the relevant information has actually survived in some form or another. The latter, and these are by far and away the most interesting, human aspects of archaeology, are fraught with problems and controversy. Concepts such as social context – and by that I mean the organization and even the ideology of an ancient society – are very nebulous and depend to an extent on each archaeologist's individual perspective; no two archaeologists will ever agree.

I have been working within sight of Peterborough cathedral since 1971 and have, I think, begun to understand the region better than most; accordingly I believe strongly that long-term regional research is the only way to understand changing ancient social 'context'. The regional approach is nothing new to British archaeology: Sir Cyril Fox carried out a superb survey of the Cambridge region in the early 1920s, but it is time-consuming. Traditionally archaeologists have studied particular classes of sites – say hillforts or long barrows – often of the same archaeological type and period but over a very wide area, such as Britain or Europe. In my view, however, this approach only allows one to skate over the surface. The usual end-result is a well-reasoned scheme of classification that often ignores the central problem of why the sites in question were constructed and used in the first place.

Archaeology is a humanity, not a science, and its great strength is that it allows us to examine past communities in time-depth: we can observe their origins, development and often their decline; but given the constraints of research funding, this is best achieved on a local or regional scale. Sadly, European prehistory has generally been studied on a piecemeal site-by-site basis and this very bitty information has been used to paint the larger picture. Very few people have been prepared to devote years of study to a specific area on the off-chance that it might provide the depth of information required to draw wider conclusions.

Recently long-running regional studies have demonstrated that they can completely overturn conventional wisdom, even if they take place in such seemingly out-of-the-way places as the Rhine delta, Fenland, Dartmoor, Somerset or County Mayo. These regional studies will provide the in-depth, reliable social and environmental contexts on which tomorrow's archaeology will be based.

The earliest landscape

The onset of the Neolithic period, around 4500 BC, saw the earliest farming in Britain. The period used to be considered as remarkably uniform, with people all over Britain living a life that was essentially the same: small, log cabin-style, pioneering peasantry who kept a few cattle, sheep or goats in paddocks, with perhaps semi-domesticated pigs scuffling around in the nearby forest, and small plots of wheat and barley nearer the homestead.

Today scientific techniques such as pollen analysis are showing that the picture is far more diverse: to take an obvious example, Caroline Malone in her companion book in the present series on Avebury, is dealing with the landscape of the rolling chalk Marlborough Downs. Except for the valley bottoms, this could not be more dissimilar to the Fenland: downland is calcareous, freely-draining and undulating, whereas the Fen can be very acidic, is sometimes actually non-draining – and is, to all intents and purposes, flat.

The economy of the very first first farmers of the Avebury region relied to a considerable extent on cereals, and indeed the small log cabin style of life is probably appropriate there. Cereals may have been grown along the Fengate fen-edge in the earliest Neolithic, but convincing evidence is very hard to come by: common sense, if nothing else, would suggest that so wet an environment, where hay and grazing were abundantly available along the water's edge, might best be suited to the rearing of livestock.

How did farming – whether of livestock, cereals or both – arrive in Britain? Was it an idea that spread, or was there a major folk movement into the British Isles shortly before 4500 BC? In some respects this is one of the most important questions in British prehistory, because the Neolithic sees the introduction not just of farming, but also of settled life and of significant new technologies that required the ability to control and direct fire – which ultimately lead to the adoption of metalworking. In essence the Neolithic sees the very beginnings of societies that had significant technological aspects in common with our own. Twenty years ago archaeologists talked about a 'Neolithic Revolution', at least as significant as the Industrial Revolution of the eighteenth and nineteenth centuries; today it is hard not to share that view, but we must not forget that the earlier 'revolution' took very much longer than the 100-odd years of the Industrial Revolution. Moreover in some areas, such as the Fenland, the old pre-Neolithic ways may have hung on far longer than in others, and for very good reasons.

The various aspects of plant and animal husbandry that together formed the Neolithic mixed farming, technology and perhaps language 'package', ultimately arrived in Britain sometime around or just after 4500 BC. The 'package' came together in the Near East and then spread across Europe, from 6000 BC, by a mechanism that nobody properly understands, even today. As it spread, it changed as it came into contact with different people and local conditions. There does seem evidence to suggest that actual populations of people were moving, but perhaps not as simple trekkers: the 'wave of advance' is too slow for that. It would seem more likely that the process involved gradual colonization, with people setting up new farms alongside their old ones as new generations were born; perhaps people moved further afield as old land became exhausted. That at least is one current explanation, but many others are possible.

The country around the fringes of Europe, however, especially the Atlantic and North Sea coasts and Scandinavia, is less accessible and less readily susceptible to the introduction of simple mixed farming. So it seems that in these regions the idea of farming arrived more slowly and piecemeal; by the same token, general trends are hard to discern. In Denmark, for example, it has been suggested that the huge blanketing forests were slowly cleared not to provide fields for cereal crops, but to give livestock good, safe grazing around watering-places. These cleared areas were slowly enlarged over the years, and the land was kept clear by grazing and browsing animals. Pigs can have a devastating effect on forests as they scuff up the ground around trees and it is probable that they were used to clear the trees – using pigs in this way would certainly take less effort than axe-felling.

Similar processes might well have operated in suitable parts of 'fringe' Britain, such as Fenland. This piecemeal view of the Neolithic 'revolution' also implies that there might well have been more involvement of the original, native, hunter-gatherer population. At this point it would be as well to note that the English Channel only formed around 5500 BC; as recently as 7000 BC the hunters and gatherers of East Anglia could have chased their game far out into the watery plains that are now covered by the North Sea. Indeed, modern trawlers have dredged-up bone and antler spearheads of this period below several fathoms of water.

Recent research into the pre-Neolithic environment of the southern Fenland has shown that areas of woodland were cleared of trees, probably by man. Such clearings were favoured by hunters as animals would be attracted there to eat the tender young shoots of rapidly regenerating plants; once in the clearing, the animals could be seen clearly and be taken with some ease. This way of life is not very different from the type of forest animal husbandry we have suggested might have taken place in early Neolithic Denmark and there is no need necessarily to suggest a wholesale change of population from the outset. Things seem to have evolved slowly. Indeed, many of the ideas and beliefs of the original, hunter-gatherer, population must have been taken up by the Neolithic newcomers as the two societies grew together.

The earlier Neolithic way of life in Fenland must have been essentially mobile, just like its Mesolithic hunting forerunner, although instead of following game, people and herds moved from one clearing to another, as grazing became exhausted. Does this then make our first farmers nomads? The answer to this must depend on what one means by the term 'nomad'. Anthropologists assure us that no people on earth have ever wandered the face of the planet completely unfettered by any territorial constraint – the definition of the true nomad. Even the inhabitants of the Steppes had to respect each others' tribal boundaries and their apparently free wandering did in fact conform to an admittedly very large-scale circuit that took advantage of different seasonal resources.

Regular seasonal movement, in which the whole or a significant part of a society move camp, is termed transhumance. By and large modern society has ceased to be transhumant, but in the past there was nearly always a degree of mobility in most societies. The shifting was always cyclical and confined within strict territorial boundaries. Today old patterns of seasonal activity may often be reflected in the shape of parish boundaries which in certain areas, such as river valleys, the fen-edge or the foothills of mountains, may be long and thin. Long, thin parishes would include upland summer grazing, dry valley-side land for crops, and marsh areas for winter protein (fish, wildfowl), lush hay, peat and firewood. In these circumstances, everybody knew where it was safe to go and people were able to exploit a range of environments with absolute security. Today the only common remnant of this ancient way of life is the seasonal movement of sheep onto high moorland pastures after spring lambing in dales and glens.

The Mesolithic hunters and gatherers were mobile and most probably operated within quite large territories. Perhaps each band of people had the use of a few fen islands, some open water, the Fen-edge and perhaps even parts of the higher hinterland. Doubtless, too, the territories were disputed from time to time and children would have been brought up to respect the edges of their daily world. Slowly, as the Neolithic way of life developed, and people began to exploit the landscape more efficiently, so territories became smaller. The population grew and inevitably disputes between different groups became more frequent; in these circumstances it would become necessary to organize the landscape more thoroughly, with clear markers and boundaries, so that everyone literally knew where they stood. Society too would have to organize and formalize its lines of communication between different groups and indeed between different generations. In short, societies were becoming more structured and better integrated.

Now the precise origin of the first Neolithic settlers in Fenland is a matter of hot debate: did they come from southern England, or did they come directly across the North Sea, from Holland? Or did they come from both directions? My own preference is for the last explanation, but with a stronger bias in favour of the Low Countries than southern England. The main reason for this is that the two types of countryside across the North Sea are so similar and require a very highly adapted type of Neolithic economy to be managed effectively.

Professor Louwe-Kooijmans of Leiden University in Holland carried out an extraordinarily detailed study of the prehistory of a part of the wet and low-lying Rhine/Meuse delta region. He was able to show how even the smallest natural islands were lived-on and that the wetland was far from uninhabited and desolate. Whilst carrying out this research he noted that certain Neolithic pots from low-lying and wet sites in Holland strongly resembled those from contemporary low-lying wet sites in eastern England. Now one must not read too much into a few pieces of broken pottery, but the topographical positions of the two groups of sites were so similar that it seemed to be more than just coincidence. Of course we cannot be certain, but contacts across the North Sea were to continue throughout the Bronze Age and I am convinced that Professor Louwe-Kooijmans was right, and that these contacts were first established in the earlier Neolithic. At Flag Fen we continue the tradition of social contact by employing his excellent students on a regular basis.

So to sum up: we currently believe that the Fen-edge landscape was first occupied by people living a broadly Neolithic way of life sometime before 4000 BC – although there is little direct evidence for this. We also suspect that these communities were ethnically related to the Mesolithic hunter-gatherers of earlier times and that their very mobile way of life predominantly revolved around animal husbandry, but within clearly understood tribal territories.

We will now examine the evidence on the ground and see how this supports some of the theories. We will start with a site excavated in the late 1960s before I personally became

23 *Aerial photograph of Fengate showing the clear crop-mark of a ditched rectangular enclosure, later known as Fengate Site 11. (Cambridge University Collection; copyright reserved.)*

involved with the area.

Fengate Site 11

This site has been destroyed by the foundations of a diesel engine testing factory built in the late 1960s. Before work began, however, local archaeologists were able to carry out a rapid excavation. Aerial photographs showed that the area to be built-on was covered by the cropmarks of a rather odd-looking, but very carefully laid-out rectangular ditch (**23**).

Excavations were carried out in 1968, but on a very small scale, and this inevitably meant that it was difficult to appreciate the ancient landscape which gave the site its physical context; indeed, given the constraints under which they had to operate, it is a wonder that the excavators of 'Site 11' made any sense of it at all. With the vantage of hindsight (not to mention eight years of excavation), we can now see that this, the first excavation of Fengate after the Second World War, was of perhaps its most ancient remains.

We have seen in the previous chapter that the site was named 'Site 11' after the Royal Commission Peterborough Volume that had then just been published. It is well known that aerial photographs only reveal a small fraction of the buried ancient remains – often just the deepest pits and ditches – and Site 11 was to prove no exception. The rectangular ditch enclosed an area of about 50 m by 30 m (165 x 99 ft) and within it there was a scatter of

24 *Foundation trenches of a small rectangular Early Neolithic 'house' (2 m (6½ ft) scale).*

post-holes. The ditch, however, was peculiar from a number of points of view: first, drainage ditches of farms, yards and gardens have to be maintained in a good state. Once they become clogged with silt and vegetation they cease to function properly and must then be redug or cleaned out (in the Fens it is called 'slubbing out' and the stagnant black mud is the 'slub'). The Site 11 enclosure ditch was quite big: some 3 m (10 ft) wide and about 70 cm (27 in.) deep, but there were no signs whatsoever of maintenance; it was dug once, and that was that. Indeed, there were some indications that it might even have been filled in deliberately.

Secondly, there was no sign of an entrance-way. Normally speaking, one would expect the ditch to be broken somewhere, so that people or animals could have access to the interior. This ditch, however, was continuous. Strangely, too, there were signs of a bank on the

inside edge of the ditch. If this was a domestic site one would hardly throw up a bank to prevent water draining into the ditch from the roofs of buildings enclosed by it; normally one would expect such a bank on the outside of an enclosure ditch. It was also laid out, as the aerial photograph makes clear, in a very strict rectangle, with sharp corners and straight sides. This again hinted at a single period of use, as sharp corners tend to get rounded and straight ditches bent, once they become subject to regular maintenance.

Archaeologists, like other people, invoke the Almighty when they are in a tight spot; thus otherwise inexplicable sites are assigned a 'ritual' or religious function when all else fails. Site 11 is such a site, but in this case it is also probably the truth, as there are good 'contextual' arguments to support this explanation. We currently believe that Site 11 had something to do with the disposal of the dead, despite the fact that no bodies were found there. But to explain this we must move forward to 1972, the second season of the main Fengate

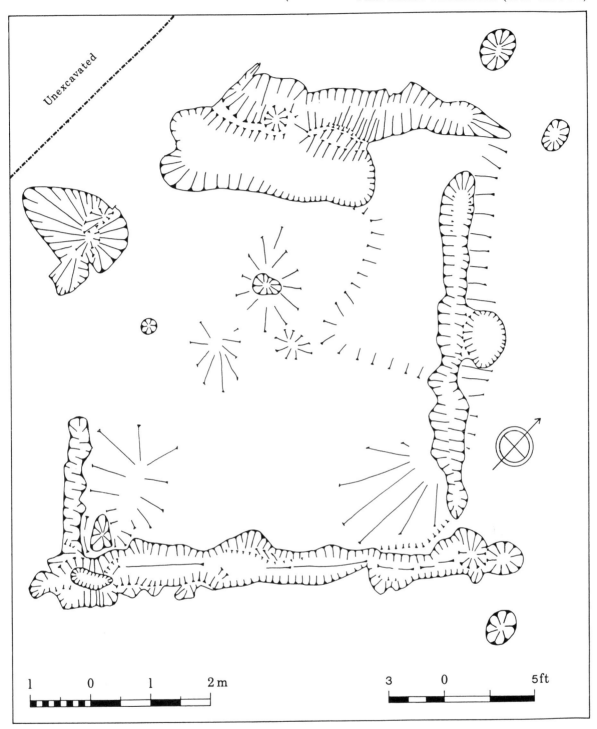

25 *Plan of the foundation trenches of the small rectangular Early Neolithic 'house'. The small circular pits within and outside the building were probably contemporary with it.*

47

excavation, then we will return to Site 11.

The Padholme Road 'house' and multiple burial

The summer of 1972 had long hot spells, and these made the recognition of buried ancient features a hit-and-miss affair. In Fengate we had a rough rule of thumb that the earlier the buried feature, the paler the soil that filled it. Roman ditches often revealed themselves, once the topsoil had been removed, as sharp black marks on the stripped surface, but features three thousand years older were very pale indeed and could be extremely hard to distinguish from the undisturbed subsoil around them.

One of the great advantages of using earthmoving machines to expose archaeological sites is that they work quickly; this means that there is more damp soil exposed at any one time, and experience has shown that soil colours show up best when damp. I remember well when we were working on the Padholme Road sub-site and the sun was blazing; no

matter how fast the machine worked, the soil swiftly dried to a uniform palish brown. Then one day the sky darkened and we prepared ourselves for a very heavy thunderstorm. The ground did need wetting, but heavy storms smudge and obliterate; so we sat in the site hut mentally preparing ourselves for two or three days' tedious re-hoeing.

I have often observed that the tall brick factory chimneys that cluster around Peterborough can have a weird affect on the weather: storms seem to be heading straight at one, then they swerve away at the last minute. That is what happened in this case: the storm seemed to swing to one side and we were lightly caressed by about ten minutes of steady rain. It was ideal. I ran to the edge of the trench and

26 *Close-up of the rib-cage of a man, aged about 35, from a multiple burial of the Early Neolithic period. A leaf-shaped flint arrowhead lies lodged between the eighth and ninth ribs.*

looked down; there in the freshly moistened ground was a distinctly darker impression of a roughly rectangular small ditch or gully. As I watched, it began to fade, so we rapidly scratched its outline in the soil with our trowels, and by the end of the day the lines were sun-baked hard; nothing could shift them now.

We knew from the pale filling of the ditch that this was something early in date and our suspicions were confirmed when we began to find long, thin, blade-like flints protruding above the surface. These blades were entirely typical of the earlier Neolithic flint-working technology and I was well pleased. It seemed to me that we had the foundation trenches of a pioneering farmer's small house (24). Houses of this period are very rare indeed in Britain, and the Fengate example seemed more-or-less the same as the four or five others known at the time, so the explanation seemed reasonable.

The foundation trenches enclosed an area that measured 7 x 8.6 m (23 x 27 ft) and showed signs of having been rebuilt or repaired at least once (25). The contents included a few very soft fragments of pottery which were quite finely-finished and one sherd showed that the potter had burnished the vessel's inside lip with a lightly-executed fluted design. Delicate fluting of this sort is very characteristic of English earlier Neolithic pottery. The foundation trenches also produced many dozens of flint implements and the by-products of their man-ufacture – small flakes, spalls and bashed pieces. Among the flints were so-called 'serrated blades'; these were long thin flakes of flint with serrations as fine as a coarse breadknife; invariably the serrated cutting edge showed a clear, bright polish when held up to the light. This polish, or 'lustre' is generally thought to be the result of cutting cereals, grasses or reeds. The small individual serrated blades were pro-bably mounted together in a piece of bone or wood to make a composite sickle.

The conventional view of the Neolithic econ-omy relies to a great extent on the use of grain. I have said that this may well have been exaggerated in the case of Fengate, but there was nonetheless good indirect evidence for it: a beautifully made, but broken, single-piece flint sickle. The site had more surprises in store: near the end of the excavation we found a large flake of polished greenstone that had been deliberately struck off a polished stone axe.

The stone used to make the axe derived from known Neolithic quarries on the other side of the country at Langdale in Cumbria. The most unusual find, however, was quite small and seemingly insignificant. It was a polished jet bead with a low collar at each end and a hole running through the middle. At some point this cherished item had split straight down the middle, but instead of throwing it away the owner had carefully (but rather crudely) chipped another small hole, thereby converting the split half-bead into a sort of toggle.

Archaeological opinion generally agreed with my interpretation that the site was a house, albeit a very early one, and there the matter rested. Indeed, we wrote it up as a house and nobody objected. Then three years later (1975) we were excavating in the Cat's Water sub-site, about 200 m (660 ft) to the south-east, when the site supervisor, David Cranstone, was not satisfied that he had reached the bottom of an Iron Age ditch. It was late summer and I planned to close the dig down the following week. So when David made his announcement I was less than happy. I simply wanted a quick and straightforward end to the season. Still, he insisted and I acceded with bad grace.

Down he dug, day after day and nothing was found, just bucketful after bucketful of clean silt; my patience was becoming somewhat strained when he appeared holding a single flint flake. I have to say that my delight at this discovery was not unreserved, for the simple reason that single flint flakes are hardly a rare occurrence at Fengate. If one swallow does not make a summer, one flint does not justify several days' hard work. A few moments later I heard a whoop of satisfaction: at the bottom of his by now huge hole he had come across human bones. When cleaned up, the pit could be seen to contain the crouched body of a young man who had been killed by an arrow whose leaf-shaped flint head still lay lodged between his eighth and ninth ribs (26). At his feet were the jumbled bones of an infant and a child and beyond them were the bones of a young woman. It is tempting to see this as a family group, but it is hard to imagine the tragedy that overtook them.

The arrowhead was of a characteristically early Neolithic type, and although one must not make such wild assertions, I thought at the time that the family might well have lived in the house nearby. By now we were running

27 *The bodies in the Early Neolithic pit grave were lifted from the ground entire, by embedding the bones in plastic. They are now on display in Peterborough Museum.*

very short of time, but I felt that this early homicide (it is among the earliest in Britain) was too important to disturb. So we lifted the group intact in two large blocks, and they can now be seen on display in Peterborough Museum (**27**).

The season of 1972 was rather frantic, as factories were being built all around us, and we did not wish to delay their construction. I know it is easy to take a purist line and tell the world to go its own way while we get on with the archaeology, but in the early 1970s unemployment in Britain was high and I did not feel too happy about causing undue delay to projects that would ultimately affect local employment. So we worked in several areas at once, and I am proud to say we never caused any factory development to fall behind schedule on our behalf only.

The Neolithic 'house' was on the Padholme Road sub-site, but we were also digging a large trench on the Vicarage Farm sub-site, almost 1.6 km (1 mile) to the west. The subsoil here was mainly limestone and it had been quite seriously affected by modern deep ploughing. Most of the features were Iron Age (see chapter 6), except for two parallel ditches which ran diagonally across the trench. These ditches were almost devoid of finds, except for a few flints and a fragment of polished stone axe, again from the ancient quarries at Langdale, Cumbria. Another Langdale axe fragment was found in a pit nearby. So, with the large Langdale flake from the 'house', the Fengate excavations of 1972 had produced no less than three flakes from a source over 480 km (300 miles) away. It looked more than probable that the two ditches that ran diagonally across the Vicarage Farm sub-site were indeed Neolithic in date. But what on earth were they doing there?

In fact, by the end of the 1975 season when

we found the multiple burial we had discovered all the main elements of an early Neolithic landscape, but we did not realize it. It took twelve more years for the penny to drop. When eventually it did descend, it happened, like most worthwhile discoveries, entirely by accident. The key to understanding the discoveries of 1972 and 1975 lay in the writing-up of the Site 11 excavations of 1968. So now I will return to the theme that I began earlier.

I was approached by administrators at English Heritage to write a report on the Site 11 excavations of 1968 that had been carried out under the auspices of the Department of Public Buildings and Works, a branch of central government that was a forerunner of English Heritage; I agreed, but reluctantly, as it is always difficult to interpret someone else's notes, no matter how good they may be.

I worked my way slowly through the Site 11 notebooks and plans, trying to get a feel for the dig. Then gradually it dawned on me that the neatly rectangular ditched enclosure was not Early Bronze Age, as had previously been thought, but very much earlier – early Neolithic, in fact. I put the idea to Dr Ian Kinnes at the British Museum, today a foremost authority in the field and by chance a supervisor on the original excavation, and he agreed. We are now both convinced that the enclosure had a funerary function and our interpretation is now supported by the recent excavation of a closely similar site at Rivenhall in Essex; this is also of Neolithic date, and is interpreted as a funerary site, with good evidence. This explanation would account for the Fengate enclosure's strict shape, lack of obvious signs of maintenance and general lack of household rubbish.

Having decided that Site 11 was older than we had previously thought, I then drew up a map of the various fragments of earlier Neolithic landscape that we either knew about or suspected. To my surprise Site 11 shared the same orientation and approximate alignment

as the Padholme Road 'house'. So was it a family house or a mortuary house? Given the high quality of the material from its foundation trenches, together with its general resemblance to other, known, mortuary structures, I am now firmly of the opinion that the 'house' is closely connected with Site 11 and that both are concerned with death.

Neither site produced actual skeletons, but that is not particularly unusual, as they may have been used to house bodies temporarily. Perhaps the jumbled bones in the large multiple grave were stored in such a place to await the death of the young man, at which point the family was finally re-united. I do not think it is a coincidence that the large grave pit is located so close to the 'house'.

I consulted the map and immediately saw that the Site 11 enclosure has precisely the same orientation as the Vicarage Farm parallel ditches. The pieces of the puzzle were now falling in place: it would seem that the landscape of the early third and later fourth millennia BC at Fengate was far from haphazard. We had lost most of the physical remains of the landscape, but what did survive was internally consistent. Although made almost a decade after the completion of the Fengate project and without any digging whatsoever, the discovery of this, one of the earliest landscapes in Britain, was a great revelation. And immensely satisfying. It shows that archaeological discoveries are not only made with a spade and trowel.

One final point arose from this latest research: if one plots the orientation of the earlier Neolithic landscape and compares it with that of the next, mainly Bronze Age, landscape, the two are clearly dissimilar (see **28**). The earlier landscape does not respect (i.e. run at right-angles to) the nearby fen, whereas the Bronze Age landscape does. The reason for this is elegant: the nearby fen had not yet formed by the earlier Neolithic, whereas by the early Bronze Age, as we shall shortly see, it was a force that could not be ignored.

4
The earlier Bronze Age (2000-1000 BC)

The three-Age system of Stone followed by Bronze and Iron was originally intended to classify museum collections. Although invented in 1836 in Denmark, it has served us well, but now, it must be admitted, it is beginning to show its age. There are many reasons for this, not the least being that the transitions between the various Ages do not always happen at times when society itself was undergoing significant change. Furthermore, the recent tendency amongst archaeologists to examine the development of entire landscapes often means that major changes can be seen to take place slowly; our view of prehistory is less like a ladder with neat rungs and more like a clambering vine: you select the strands that seem interesting and follow them wherever they may lead. Given this view of the past, the transition from the Stone Age to the Bronze Age is highly significant if one is examining, for example, the development of axe-blade technology, but less so if one is concerned with the development of the landscape as a whole.

The discovery of the Bronze Age field system

The previous chapter discussed the earlier Neolithic period and we saw that the organization of the landscape was already beginning. We still have no hard evidence for the details of the way of life of its inhabitants, but we know they were farmers and we may safely assume that by the end of the period, let us say around 2500 BC, the phase of mobility was drawing to a close. People were settling down and the landscape had acquired structure and permanence.

We do not know what happened in the centuries at the close of the third millennium BC (i.e.

shortly before 2000 BC) at Fengate, but it was probably important since it led to the abandonment of the existing landscape. The next development we can see is the laying-out of an entirely new landscape, as we have already noted on a different orientation from that which had gone before; and this time the orientation of the landscape respected the existence of the emerging wetland to the east (28).

Some archaeologists like to play down the excitement of their work: nothing must appear unexpectedly and everything must be anticipated. Speaking for myself, there is nothing I enjoy more than when the truth creeps up and knocks all one's cherished ideas for six. This first happened to me in 1971.

I had ordered a set of Professor St Joseph's aerial photographs from Cambridge, including ones that were not printed in the Royal Commission 'Peterborough Volume'. I laid them out on the floor of my flat while my wife was out of the room. There was a shout that the potatoes needed turning down, so I dutifully got up and left the room. I returned a few minutes later and the low evening sun had moved slightly. Maybe it was something else, but as I stood looking down at the photos I noticed a series of parallel lines in the cropmarks that positively leapt out at me. Almost every photo had its set of these paired ditches (see 12 and 13).

The 'Peterborough Volume' was hurriedly consulted and it was apparent that Chris Taylor had also noted some, but by no means all of the ditches, which were circumspectly described as 'trackways' and of uncertain date, but possibly Roman. One of the photos on my floor clearly showed a 'trackway' to be overlain by a Roman road of known early date. The 'trackways' had, therefore, to be prehistoric. (I suspect by now

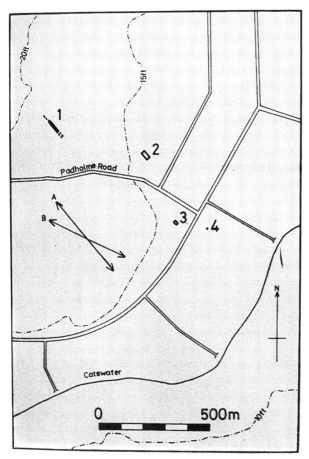

28 *The changing alignment of the Neolithic and Bronze Age landscapes at Fengate. (1) the Vicarage Farm paired ditches; (2) Site 11; (3) the Padholme Road 'house'; (4) the Cat's Water multiple burial; (A) the earlier Neolithic landscape alignment; (B) the later Neolithic and Bronze Age landscape.*

the potatoes had boiled dry.)

The next morning earthmoving machines were arriving on site for the second time that season, and I determined that we should take a look at the supposedly Roman 'trackway' ditches (**29**). The first thing that struck me when we had removed the overburden was that the material filling the ditches was very pale – had they been Roman it would have been much darker. So we opened a few hand-cut sections and found that the finds from within the ditch filling were very few and far between – again, not something characteristic of Roman ditches

in the area. It must have been another two or three weeks before we came across anything diagnostic from the ditches, in this case two fired clay cylindrical weights, which might originally have been used for tensioning a loom or sinking fishing nets. Cylindrical weights of this sort are very typical of the later Bronze Age, and are never found on Roman sites. Things were beginning to take shape.

After the 1972 season we all accepted the idea that the 'trackways' were Bronze Age, but we still had no idea of their role or purpose. For a while we considered the suggestion that they might have been defensive – a sort of Fenland equivalent of the ditches around Maiden Castle – but we soon rejected the idea as manifestly absurd: they were going *from* nowhere *to* nowhere and defended nothing.

Storey's Bar Way sub-site

The following season (1973) we started work on the Storey's Bar Way sub-site (see **18**). The aerial photograph showed a few ditches, but chief among them was a large ring-ditch with a dark patch on one side – rather like a precious stone setting on a finger-ring (see **12** and **13**). The normal procedure in such cases has always been to treat the ring-ditch as if it were the ditch encircling a Bronze Age round barrow. Barrows are usually fairly complex sites and are therefore often excavated on their own, in splendid isolation, largely to minimize the complexity. Armed with the confidence bestowed by lack of experience I decided to approach this one differently and to treat it as if it were part of a much larger landscape. We therefore decided to strip topsoil from most of the modern field and see what lay around it.

At that time a friend of mine was the manager of a local plant-hire firm and he was also keenly interested in archaeology. He was therefore able to offer me a range of machines at very competitive rates indeed. We had a wonderful time, using all sorts of peculiar equipment in the most improbable ways, and I was able to put together a small booklet on earthmoving as a result. I also got to drive anything I wanted – which has proved a very useful skill subsequently.

After six weeks of earthmoving we had cleared a large area so efficiently that we did not need to hoe the surface (see **16**). The ring-ditch was clearly visible, but near it (and not discernible on the air photos) were much

29 *Bronze Age 'trackway' ditches 1 and 2 during excavation (Fengate, 1972). These parallel ditches bounded a droveway in a large system of fields and paddocks which was laid out along the flood-free land of the fen-edge.*

smaller ditches filled with pale soil (**30**). We excavated these and found they contained flints and pottery of Late Neolithic type. The pottery was not in the Peterborough tradition, as might be expected, but belonged to a uniquely British style of the same period (about 2000 BC), known as Grooved Ware (**31**). Grooved Ware is usually associated with the great 'henge' monuments of Wessex – sites such as Durrington Walls, Stonehenge itself and Avebury – and is not particularly common on domestic sites in southern Britain.

The Fengate Grooved Ware site consisted of two large ditched fields to one side of the ring-ditch; at the opposite end of the site, grouped around a 'sock' well (**32**) was a collection of small scoops and hollows, many of which

contained Grooved Ware. Presumably this was the living area. The shallow ditches that marked out the edges of the fields or paddocks usually had gaps, or entranceways, at the corners. Anyone who has kept or managed livestock will know that it is far easier to drive animals through a corner gate than through one in the long side of a field. For these and other reasons we began to suspect that these particular fields were used to hold animals, rather than crops.

The ring-ditch turned out to have a longer and more complex story than we had first suspected. It was initially dug in the Late Neolithic period by the Grooved Ware-using community and it probably surrounded a small shrine or a sacred area of some sort. It was re-dug in the Early Bronze Age, some 500 years later, to provide the material for a large earthen mound in which were housed small cremations; two young people were also buried in the re-cut ditch. The final stage of use was probably not connected with the former two. The large pit was excavated, perhaps to quarry gravel, sometime around 1000 BC. It was dug nearly 2 m (6½ ft) deep, well below the water-table, to a seam of clean gravel. Eventually the pit was abandoned and allowed to fill with stagnant muddy water and in this oozy material we found the remains of a notched alder log ladder that had presumably been used by the Bronze Age quarrymen for access to the pit.

The fields at Storey's Bar Way were then amongst the oldest known in England and we were all very excited by their discovery, but we were surprised that they were on their own: normally fields go with other fields and form part of a much larger system. Then one evening back in Toronto I was drawing up plans of the previous season's work when I noticed that the Grooved Ware fields were laid out more-or-less parallel to the later, Bronze Age, 'trackways'.

30 *Excavations on the Storey's Bar Way sub-site (1973) revealed a ring-ditch with a large quarry pit and, beyond, the straight ditches of a field-system belonging to the Late Neolithic period.*

One should not read too much into such things, which could, of course, be entirely coincidental, but the germ of an idea was born: perhaps the 'trackways' formed part of a field system that was both larger and very much longer-lived than anything we had ever suspected?

Land-management in Bronze Age Fengate

When we excavated the 'trackway' ditches in 1972 we had made the great mistake of treating them as trackways; in other words our trenches followed along their alignment. Consequently we only found what we were looking for: trackways, which looked rather unconvincing. It is a fact not always appreciated, but archaeological interpretation is often based on circular argument and the secret of progress is to break the cycle by doing the unexpected. So in 1974 I decided to excavate across, rather than along two sets of 'trackways' in the Newark Road sub-site. Crop-marks on the aerial photo were partially obscured by river-borne flood clay and were not particularly informative; so I decided on the crude but effective technique of stripping

31 *Typical finds from the Late Neolithic site on Storey's Bar Way: the arrowhead has a single large barb and might have been used to hunt fish.*

almost the entire field, but over three consecutive seasons, 1974, 1975 and 1976. For the sake of simplicity we will consider the three together.

It was a huge earthmoving operation, as the alluvial clay on the surface was thicker than anticipated. At first we could see nothing, but gradually the outline of a massive ditch began to be revealed as we slowly worked our way down towards the gravel. The 'trackway' explanation which originally seemed so odd turned out to be reasonably accurate, since the parallel ditches ran on either side of a ribbon of land along which livestock were driven. In Fenland this type of track, running down to the wet from the dry is generally known as a 'drove'. At Fengate there are four modern roads known as the First, Second, Third and Fourth Droves, two (and I suspect this would apply to the others, did we but know it) run parallel to their prehistoric forebears. This is not continuity in the strict sense (when property boundaries are handed-on unchanged from one generation to another), but rather it reflects the fact that people living on the flood-free higher land must always have needed access to the Fen for their livestock and other farm traffic. If the folk farming the very edge of the Fen were unfriendly or greedy it would make excellent sense, and would avoid conflict, if everyone in the community recognized that access along the droves was open to anyone. It would also make sense if those access routes were as direct as possible. This is why the prehistoric and modern droves run at strict right-angles to the Fen.

This seemed an excellent working hypothesis, but I had to prove it somehow. I by then had the very good fortune to come across Dr Paul Craddock who had just started working for the British Museum Research Laboratory – where he is now a senior scientist. At the time we were both interested in the analysis of Bronze Age metal, for the information it could provide on trade and metalworking technology. I invited Paul to Canada to analyse some of the Royal Ontario Museum's British bronzes, and while he was there he casually mentioned that he had a cheap and foolproof method for doing soil phosphate analyses; I was wildly excited at this. The reason for my excitement is that when farm animals defaecate or urinate they enrich the soil with organic phosphates; if the soil conditions are right, then the phosphate molecules lock-in to the soil particles around them and stubbornly refuse to budge. If one has access, as I did, to an analytical chemist then the soil phosphate level can be measured at one spot – the Bronze Age droveway surface in our case – and compared with the land around it. Paul Craddock equipped us with a

mini-phosphate laboratory on site, courtesy of the British Museum, and we set to work.

The results showed that the surface of the ground between the droveway ditches held a higher concentration of phosphate than the land around. This was self-explanatory: more animals were going about their business there; but when we analysed soil from the sides of the droveway ditches we found that there was more phosphate along the top, or brink, than at the bottom. This was puzzling, but consistent, all along the ditches. It soon became apparent that the expected pattern of high phosphate along the bottom of a ditch would be the result of rapid run-off caused by poor drainage. Imagine a well-turfed and grassy droveway used by animals: the dung would remain on the turf until it rained, when it would be washed into the ditch – at which point it would 'fix' into the soil at the bottom. But if, as we strongly suspected from a wealth of other evidence (the number of animal bones found, the frequent modification of field entranceways and the regular recutting of ditches), the droveway surface was worn bare by the constant passage of

32 *Bottom of a Bronze Age (c.1000 BC) 'sock' well showing the wattle-work lining in place. Notice the strengthening timber across the centre. The depth of the well was about 2 m (6½ ft).*

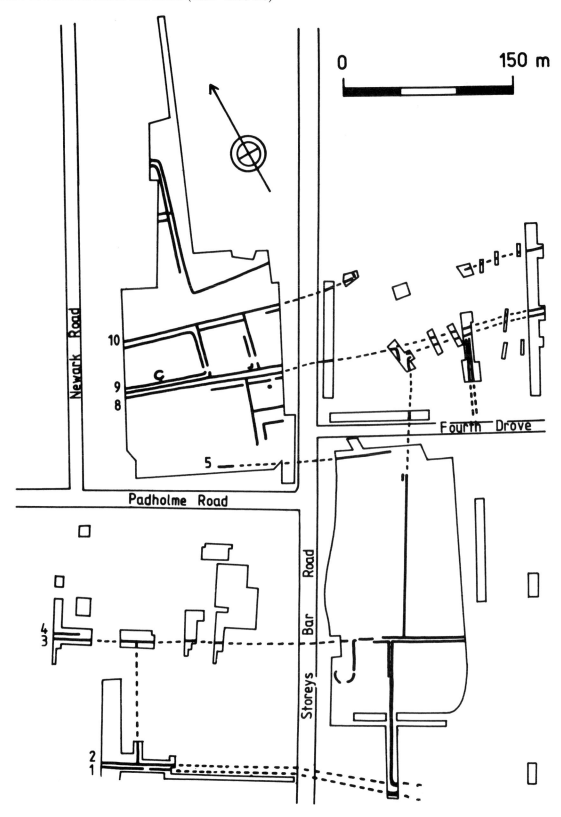

33 *Plan of the principal Fengate field ditches before the discoveries of the Power Station sub-site. (Robert Powell.)*

livestock, then there would be no turf to prevent the phosphates in the dung being absorbed directly into the soil. When it rained, the surface would absorb the water and become a smelly, muddy mess, familiar to anyone who has lived on a farm. The liquid in the slurry would soon join the water-table, which in winter would be just below the surface.

The ditches of the Newark Road sub-site formed an extraordinarily well-organized pattern, arranged around a series of droveways. We plotted the cropmarks from aerial photographs and came up with a map on which we marked and numbered the principal ditches (**33**). Only the main ditches showed up on the aerial

photos which otherwise gave no hint that the 'trackways' were linked together by many other ditches and smaller, subsidiary droves; this illustrates well the very great danger of attempting to read too much into even the very best aerial photos. The ditches we numbered 6 and 7 vanished when we actually came to look for them, so we must attribute their presence on the photo to a trick of the light, or modern disturbance that affected soil drainage. The main droveway was clearly that marked by ditches 8 and 9. It ran from east to west, across the Fourth Drove sub-site, down to the fen beyond it (**34** and **35**).

34 *The Newark Road sub-site (1976) looking eastwards towards Flag Fen in the distance. Bronze Age drove ditches 8 (right) and 9 (left) can be seen running across the excavation.*

35 *Aerial view of the Newark Road excavations, looking south-east. The Bronze Age field boundary ditches can be clearly seen. (S.J. Upex, Nene Valley Research Committee.)*

Ditches 8 and 9 were often of very variable depth, profile and width, and it soon became apparent that they had been extensively dug, redug, filled in and then opened again. In most instances these activities were connected with the making and blocking of causeways across the ditch. These causeways were usually at the corners of neighbouring fields or paddocks, just as we had seen at Storey's Bar Way. We also noticed that a causeway across Ditch 8 would

never line up with one across Ditch 9; in other words there was no evidence to suggest that people wanted to drive livestock straight across the droveway. In this respect it served as a barrier or boundary.

The fields or paddocks on either side of the droveway marked by Ditches 8 and 9 were laid out without regard to each other: not only did entranceways not line up, but neither did subsidiary droves or even field boundary ditches. The two sets of paddocks were entirely self-centred and separated from one another by the main drove. This pattern of fields has been termed 'co-axial' by Andrew Fleming who has worked on much larger and broadly contemporary field or 'Reave' systems on Dartmoor. It is generally considered that the landscape might have been divided into large areas by the main 'boundary droves'; perhaps these large areas were given to individual families and the subdivisions within them, essentially the fields and smaller, subsidiary droves, then came into being as and when required. We will see shortly that the Ditch 8 and 9 drove's role as a boundary was just as important as its more obvious 'trackway' function.

These interpretations were fine insofar as they went, but there were still some practical difficulties. For example, some of the drove and field boundary ditches were only 20–30 cm (9–12 in.) deep, when excavated. If one adds another 30 cm (1 ft) to compensate for lost topsoil and soil erosion, this still only provides a very slight obstacle for any determined cow or sheep. Add a bank of roughly the same size and it is still negligible, but plant a stout thorn hedge on top of the bank, and one will have a stock-proof barrier in 5–7 years. There is no evidence for fence posts at Fengate – and in view of the wet soil this is not surprising – so a hedge is quite simply the only way the land could have been physically divided. Having said that, it is always possible that the small ditches were merely psychological barriers, like the drove of Ditches 8 and 9; or perhaps livestock were either tethered in place, or constantly supervised by several stockmen. Personally, I find these suggestions improbable: if the small droveway ditches only served a psychological boundary function they would soon have been obliterated by wandering hooves; as it is, they are sharp and well-defined, protected, I would argue, by a physical barrier.

It has long been assumed in archaeology that

when one digs a ditch and throws the spoil to one side that the spoil will eventually slip back into the ditch when moved by rain, snow and frosts. In certain circumstances this makes sense, for example if one is building an earthen fort one tries to make the encircling bank and ditch substantial, so they are placed close to one another, and both are as steep as possible and accordingly they rapidly collapse. If, on the other hand, one is digging a ditch in the Fens one does not want to dig it out at regular intervals, so any bank is very flat and set well back from the edge of the ditch. It was not surprising, therefore that few of the Fengate ditches showed signs of bank collapse in their

infilling; but this did not mean that there were no banks.

When colleagues visited the Newark Road excavations I would point out that there was no evidence for banks, but I still stoutly maintained that they must have been there; I need hardly add that I was rarely believed. So I determined to have a serious look for them and turned my attention to the nearby Fourth Drove sub-site where the river-borne clay cover was thicker and where there was a large modern drainage dyke under whose upcast we might find what we were after.

Below the thick topsoil at the edge of the dyke we found Ditch 10 and to one side of it

36 *The buried bank of a Bronze Age field boundary ditch was found in the deeper soils of the Newark Road sub-site.*

what we had been looking for: a low, flat mound capped with gravel that had been dug from the bottom of the ditch (**36**). The mound was placed well back from the ditch by the Bronze Age farmer who plainly had had no intention of redigging it more than was absolutely necessary. The gravel on the top of the mound showed slight signs of disturbance, but one could not say with absolute confidence that this resulted from root action. However the neat and regular profile of both ditch and bank suggests actual physical protection, probably by a hedge.

37 *Foundation trenches and post-holes of an earlier Bronze Age round house, Newark Road sub-site. The four posts of the doorway and porch are in the centre foreground and the ring of roof-support posts can be clearly seen. An eaves-drip gully runs around the building and drains into a nearby field boundary ditch.*

Houses and habitations

Our excavations around the Bronze Age field system revealed the foundations of three or four Bronze Age round houses, one of which was particularly well-preserved (**37**). The building in question was on the Newark Road sub-site and had been placed in a paddock alongside Ditch 9. No wood survived, but the stains left by posts in the gravel subsoil were clearly visible. The building showed no signs of repair and probably remained in use for no more than twenty to thirty years. It consisted of an exterior eaves-drip gully (the equivalent of a gutter), a circular exterior wall with a diameter of about 8 m (26 ft) and a single, porched doorway which faced eastwards and would have allowed the inhabitants to keep an eye on animals in the adjoining two paddocks. The eaves-drip gully eventually drained into a subsidiary drain running parallel to Ditch 9.

The building had a central hearth, but its main interest lay in a series of posts which formed an internal ring of roof-supports. Bronze Age buildings often have such an internal post-

38 *The reconstruction of the earlier Bronze Age house (c.1500 BC): following the wattling of the walls, the first roof rafters are placed in position. Note the flat angle (c.35 degrees) of the roof.*

ring, and archaeologists have long been puzzled by them, for the simple reason that if the roof was thatched with reed or straw the weight (in this case about $2\frac{1}{2}$ tonnes) simply would not require additional support: Peter Reynolds' experiments at Little Butser have shown that large round houses with thick thatch and a properly constructed conical roof are perfectly stable when the weight is taken on the walls alone; internal roof-supports are therefore not needed.

We decided to resolve this problem by attempting a reconstruction, but we decided to go the whole way and actually reconstruct not just the house, but the fields and droveway, too. We would have liked to have done this on the spot where the building actually stood, but this is now occupied by a large factory. So we

bided our time and eventually obtained land at Flag Fen, just east of Fengate, and this is where we have built our experimental Bronze Age structures (**38–41**). We originally intended to go the whole way and fell every pole with Bronze Age axes, but soon gave the idea up when we came to cost the operation with more precision. So I must now confess that we compromised and felled half a dozen poles using authentic techniques, before laying our palstaves (a type of Bronze Age axe) aside, and resumed work with chain saws.

We gave a Bronze Age axe to Rodney Newborough, a senior forester with the Forestry Commission and he felled several trees of 30 cm (1 ft) diameter in about three minutes each (it takes me a good quarter of an hour). After felling three trees Rodney's bronze axe blade was still as sharp as a razor. It was most noticeable that the trees were felled well above ground level – far higher than with modern long-handled steel felling axes (**42**).

We built our first round building in 1989 and were advised on its construction by John Spencer who has built round houses all over

39 *Weaving the wattle purlins through the rafters.*

the country. Before becoming a prehistoric house-builder John worked with us on various excavations in the Peterborough area, while still a student at Manchester University. So by dint of persistent pestering, coupled with a degree of acceptable moral blackmail, we persuaded him to give us a hand. John had the idea that perhaps the ring of roof-support posts was made necessary because of the roof's weight; clearly thatch was out, and there is no suitable local stone, but what about turf? Turf-roof houses are known from northern Scotland and the Western Isles and also in Scandinavia. John calculated that our roof, when wet could weigh 7 or 8 tonnes (tons) and this would certainly require substantial support. We knew from our reading of Scottish accounts that the first layer of turf was laid green-side down, and the second was laid on it, but right-side up. Then the two grew together to make a very solid mat.

The summer of 1989 was improbably hot and dry and we only kept the roof alive by dint of assiduous sprinkling. At the end of the summer the turf had formed into a tough covering, and although I was able to walk around on it barefoot, it was by no means waterproof. We were then visited by Dr Bengt Edgren a colleague who runs a reconstructed Iron Age fort in southern Sweden and he was not surprised at our leaky roof and pointed out that theirs, which may last twenty years or more, have a straw or reed lining which channels water to the ground. The turf then serves to keep the lining in place and makes an efficient insulation – which is highly desirable in Sweden. We followed his advice and inserted a layer of second-hand thatcher's reed below the turf, and so far the experiment had proved successful. In the future we intend to keep the roof tidy by having it grazed by primitive sheep. In fact Flag Fen can now boast its own small flock of Soay sheep, a very primitive rare breed whose bones are virtually identical to those found on Neolithic and Bronze Age sites in Britain and

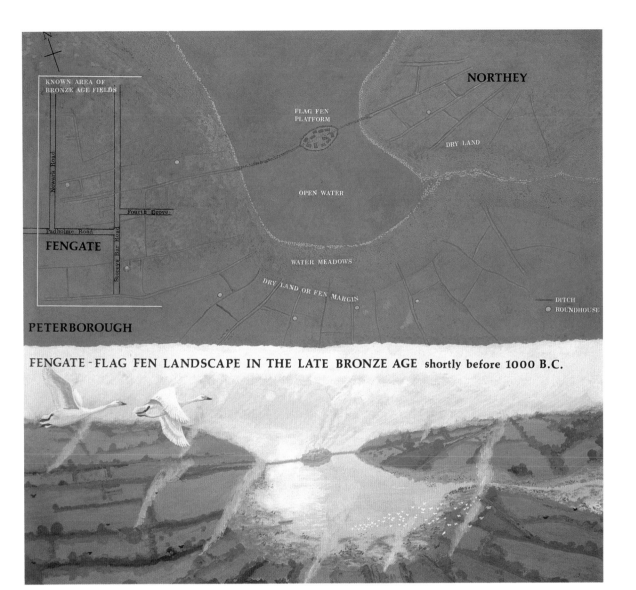

1 Two views of the Fengate and Flag Fen landscape (Chris Owen).

(above)
2 The fen-edge at Fengate,
around 1500 BC
(Rob Donaldson).

(right)
3 The first photograph of the
Flag Fen Bronze Age timbers,
immediately after their
discovery, mid-November 1982.

4 View of the excavation of Flag Fen in 1987, taken by the roof-mounted camera.

(above)

5 View along the timber uprights, showing the highest layer of horizontal wood. The oak planks in the foreground are part of the underlying floor.

(top right)

6 First exposure of the floor level timbers at Flag Fen.

(bottom right)

7 Aerial view of the highest level timbers, including a 'dump' of probably unused structural timbers (top right).

8   Ground level view of 'dump' of unused structural timbers.

9   The lowest level of foundation timber, with frequent pegs securing the main baulks of timber into position.

10 A selection of Bronze Age finds from Flag Fen 1986-89. A complete ceramic jar; decorated antler harness cheek-piece; 2 shale bracelet fragments, a bronze stick-pin and a bronze dagger (Derek Rootes).

11 A selection of Late Bronze Age weapons from Fengate Power Station, 1989. 3 swords; a rapier; 3 dirks or daggers (one with an antler handle); 2 socketed spearheads and one chape (metal tip for a sword scabbard) (Derek Rootes).

12 An artist's impression of ceremonies at the Fengate Power Station post alignment. The timber platform and buildings at Flag Fen are shown, although they would probably have been abandoned by this stage (Rob Donaldson).

Europe (**43**). It was an extraordinary sensation to be in the round-house with these, its rightful occupants; it was hard not to feel distinctly out of place.

The ditched fields of the Newark Road sub-site were of prime importance, but they had undoubtedly been slightly affected by deep ploughing in modern times, so we decided to examine the nearby Fourth Drove sub-site more closely, for here, as we have already noted, the overlying alluvial clays were very much thicker. Unfortunately we had to defer this examination until 1978, the last year of the project, which was not entirely our fault as the land was not available until then, and when we got down to the work, the sheer quantity

of overburden made 'open area' excavation impossible, given our limited budget. So we dug long keyhole trenches, about 5 m ($16\frac{1}{2}$ ft) wide and demonstrated that the whole prehistoric landscape, including the topsoil, lay below the surface, untouched, so far as we could tell, by modern ploughing. I still bitterly regret not being able to excavate Fourth Drove properly, using open area techniques, but that was the way things worked out.

In 1989 we examined the Power Station sub-site immediately to the fenward, or easterly, side of the Fourth Drove sub-site. This will be covered more fully in the next chapter, but to our absolute delight we found that our old friends Ditches 8 and 9 ran right up to the edge of the water. This was very important, for after eighteen years' research we had finally linked the dryland landscape to the Fens. It was important to us, but of greater significance to people in the Bronze Age.

40 *Placing the first roof turves in position directly on the timberwork. This was a mistake: later we had to raise all the turf and place a layer of reed beneath to lift it clear of the rafters which were showing signs of wet-rot.*

41 *Turfing nearing completion.*

42 *Artist's impression of a Late Bronze Age axeman at work, felling a tree. Note that the tree is felled well above ground level. (Jo Richards.)*

43 *When nearly completed the Fengate Bronze Age round house was used to hold a flock of Soay sheep, a rare breed thought to have its origins in the Bronze Age or Neolithic period.*

The Fenland Bronze Age

I cannot finish a discussion of the Bronze Age in the Fens without saying something about David Hall's recent discoveries. He was the first field officer with English Heritage's Fenland Project and does his fieldwork in the Cambridgeshire Fens. He started tramping across fields in 1976, to the sum of 8000 ha (20,000 acres) a year, and soon came across a series of very low gravel mounds. These mounds were in peat country near the village of Haddenham, not far from Ely. He sought an explanation for them, but as little sensible was suggested, soon came to the correct conclusion that they were in fact prehistoric barrows, or burial mounds.

In England barrows came in two main variet-ies: round (mainly Bronze Age) and long (Neolithic). The trouble is, however, that inquiring minds have always been interested in barrows, and in the not-too-distant past people were perfectly prepared to satisfy their curiosity with a spade. In the last century barrow 'opening' was a respectable occupation for churchmen who might often be found on a summer's afternoon looking on while workmen dug into some inoffensive mound; generally speaking each mound took a day or two to loot, but seldom any longer; nowadays an archaeologist would expect to spend six or more weeks excavating a barrow.

Most parts of England were ravaged by Victorian and Edwardian antiquarians and few places were too remote, be they the Marlborough Downs, the Yorkshire Dales or the Derbyshire Peaks. Sadly it is hard to think of a single area where the main barrow fields remain intact; sadly, too, the records left by the antiquarians are often lacking or woefully inadequate; in most cases the 'records' are simply the hand-written labels on the urns and other items

44 *A round barrow, probably dating to the Early Bronze Age, revealed in the side of a dyke in Borough Fen.*

that came from the ground.

So the real importance of David Hall's discovery is that whole barrowfields are now emerging, as the peaty soils 'shrink' away. But what are we to do? We cannot in all conscience dig the lot, or we will be little better than our antiquarian predecessors. On the other hand, if we do nothing the all-important organic contents of the barrows will dry up and vanish into dust. In my opinion the best preserved barrowfields, especially those around Haddenham, should be bought for the nation and then kept wet (somehow). We are currently experimenting with ways of keeping individual barrows and small barrowfields wet, using a variant of the Flag Fen lake technique.

A few barrowfields still remain wet, or damp, but others have been drained, almost beyond recall – and quite recently. The large barrowfield of Borough Fen, about 1.6 km (1 mile) north-east of Peterborough was wet in the early 1970s, but was deeply drained at the end of the decade. Today the barrows of Borough Fen appear to thrust ever higher through dry peats, and in one or two places their mounds have been cut through by drainage dykes, where we have been able to examine them more closely (**44**). It is sad to think that these monuments to our Bronze Age and Neolithic ancestors had survived largely intact for 4000 years, only to be effectively destroyed a couple of years before their significance was recognized. But to be realistic, even if their true importance had been recognized in time, the words of a few archaeologists would have had little effect on the actions of drainage authorities who had the backing of many powerful government agencies.

Archaeologists have long been fascinated by barrows. They often dominate the skyline and their brooding presence, with its all-encompassing aura of Death cannot fail to fire the imagin-

45 *Skeleton of a young woman (aged 20–23) placed at the bottom of a Bronze Age field boundary ditch.*

ation. Most Bronze Age people, however, were buried closer to home, in the fields and farms they lived in; the barrows were probably reserved for the upper classes. We found the graves of many 'ordinary' people at Fengate, some, like the young woman illustrated here (**45**) were simply laid out along the bottom of a ditch.

Life and death in the Bronze Age

So far this chapter has been concerned with the earlier Bronze Age, very approximately the years between 2000 and 1300 BC, and it will shortly be time to move on. But before we do so, we should pause and reflect on what it would have been like actually to have lived in the Fens four thousand years ago. Of course I, like any other archaeologist, have no monopoly on truth: if I could be transported back to the

earlier Bronze Age, I sometimes doubt whether the world I would see could bear any resemblance whatsoever to that in my mind's eye as I write now. Having said that, I have nothing else to go by.

During the early Neolithic period, sometime before 4000 BC, society was essentially mobile and had many points in common with the previous world of the hunter and gatherer. Then the population of the region began to grow and the separated clearings in the forests gradually expanded, coming together to form larger tracts of open countryside. By about 3000 BC there is even evidence that this early landscape was arranged into clearly defined alignments, just like many modern landscapes. This is the so-called Neolithic field system of Fengate.

The few centuries prior to 2000 BC saw the laying out of a new landscape on an entirely different alignment. This landscape was arranged along the Fen-edge and its principal elements, ditched droveways, radiated out from the wetlands at right-angles. As far as we know there were no villages, no *nucleated* settlements, to use a convenient term. People chose to live in dispersed houses, with a few outbuildings, which were dotted here and there amongst the ditched droves and paddocks (**colour plate 1**). The way of life depended to a large extent on livestock, but the rich resources of the Fen nearby were doubtless fully exploited too. I can imagine that herds of cattle might well have been led out into the Fen in dry summers to exploit the common grazing, just as happened in the Middle Ages. I also suspect that each group of people had a clear idea of where and when they could and could not graze their animals when out in the open Fen. It may have looked open, but in reality it would have been parcelled up and bounded by numerous unwritten laws.

Ten years ago when I published the Third Fengate Report, which was almost entirely devoted to the Bronze Age field and drove system, I wrote that the dispersed pattern of settlements taken with other factors such as the regular partition of the land suggested that society was relatively egalitarian. There were no obvious signs of chiefs, princes or hereditary leaders. If it was not egalitarian and leaderless, which was improbable, then its component families were fairly independent and did not support a large ruling class. I still stand by that, but with reservations, for by 1300 BC important changes were well underway; this is based on entirely new information, not available when I wrote the Third Fengate Report.

Anyone who attempts to reconstruct life in the past, and only selects mundane evidence for the humdrum and ordinary, fails to realize that life is about more than these things. I do not think that we have advanced our understanding of the past far if the best we can do is picture a Bronze Age farmer driving his cattle to Fen pastures along a hedged drove, having just eaten his breakfast of porridge from an unglazed hand-made bowl in a round house roofed with turf. I see this as merely a detailed depiction of Dr Johnson's remark that life in prehistory was 'nasty, brutish and short'. Life at any time is about living with other people and these relationships are what we must try to understand if we are to animate the Bronze Age.

Imagine our farmer trudging along the drove: was he contentedly building up his own family farm, secure in the knowledge that it would pass onto his children, or was he driving his lord and master's animals – with huge resentment? In either case mere surroundings pale into insignificance; what matters is the motive behind the action. We have established the stage and the actors – now to the play.

The generally accepted method of reconstructing lost patterns of life and social organization is to examine the anthropological record. This explains why our understanding of the way people in the Palaeolithic (Old Stone Age) period lived, is in large part based on anthropological observations of Kalahari Desert Bushmen, or tribesmen in Papua New Guinea or bands of Australian aborigines. There is nothing else to go by, so the argument goes, so we must use modern anthropological observations.

If it is hard to find anthropological parallels for Ice Age hunters, it is equally difficult to find recently-existing communities who have much in common with the Bronze Age and Neolithic of temperate Europe, and even if we could, there is absolutely no certainty that societies in either place should necessarily evolve along the same lines. Mercifully people have always behaved unpredictably, which makes archaeology so entertaining. Once we have done everything possible to extract the last drop of information from the only source we can rely on, namely, our own archaeological observations, we can then add a generous dash of anthropology, imagination and scepticism and trust that something useful might emerge by way of an intellectual cocktail.

In social terms the earlier Bronze Age was essentially a development of the later Neolithic. So far as we can tell, society became less mobile and people settled down within their appropriate tribal areas. There is evidence to suggest that some of the tribes were long-lived and treated certain sites, such as stone circles or huge tombs, as symbolic, if not actual, tribal centres; there were tribal burial areas, which we call barrowfields, and doubtless the landscape was carefully parcelled up by myriad small signs and symbols of greater or lesser importance; including family holdings, rights of way and tribal boundaries.

In some parts of England, such as Salisbury Plain, the great tribal centres of the Early Bronze Age were built of massive stones; Stonehenge and Avebury are obvious examples. Around Peterborough convenient stone is not available, so use was made of timber and probably turf, but there was no long-lived tradition of 'monumentality', of huge, spectacular and lasting centres, such as the great monuments of Wessex. Instead certain parts of the country-side were considered to be specially important and these 'ritual landscapes' as they have been unfortunately labelled, are liberally scattered with hundreds of smaller sites, such as barrows, 'henges' and numerous small family-type shrines, none of which was in use continuously for any length of time, although most show evidence for intermittent use over, perhaps, a generation or two.

The tradition of 'monumentality' never developed in lowland eastern England and it is a mistake to think of local Neolithic and Bronze Age ceremonial sites as if they were Stonehenge-like churches in which ceremonies took place. Instead, the evidence indicates that the construction and repeated reconstruction of the site was both the end and the means to it: the ceremony was the actual construction of the place in which the ceremonies took place. I do not think that once constructed the shrine (or henge to give its archaeological name) was ever subsequently 'used'.

We excavated a number of these late Neolithic and early Bronze Age religious and ceremonial sites of the Maxey 'ritual landscape' in 1986. This landscape lay in the flat, open countryside at the point where the broad lower Welland valley meets the plain around the edge of the Fen. Here one 'henge' of later Neolithic date consisted of numerous circular ditches and banks, all of different periods, which surrounded a setting of large posts.

Unless it lies destroyed beneath Peterborough – and there is no evidence to suggest this – the ceremonial tribal centre for communities living at Fengate in the late Neolithic and Early Bronze Age was in the area just discussed, around the little village of Maxey, just north of the modern city. Then in the Middle Bronze Age people stopped using barrows to cover their dead; henges went out of use and we see a new pattern emerging, all over Britain. In purely local terms we see the centre of tribal ceremonial activity shift from north of the city to its eastern Fen fringe. This change was accompanied by wetter conditions both generally and in the fen, and by the adoption of new funerary and tribal ceremonies, which were focused on the wetland.

It would be easy if the changes taking place

around and after 1300 BC (the Middle Bronze Age) could be linked to a convenient 'outside' event, but barring an undisclosed disaster of some kind, we must seek our agent of change closer to home. In the later Neolithic there is good evidence to suggest that in Wessex, if not elsewhere, society was highly stratified and there may well have been classes who did little else but maintain their own authority through religious observances, lavish funerary rituals and so on.

It is difficult to be certain, but the general run of evidence from East Anglia points to a rather different tradition, which is why I still, on the whole, stand by my original interpretation of the society behind the Fengate ditched fields as being basically egalitarian. Of course, there was a degree of social stratification in the earlier Bronze Age of the Peterborough region, but I do not believe it was either so pronounced or so well established as in Wessex. Neither the barrows, the 'henges' nor the rich burials of East Anglia are even remotely comparable with their grand contemporaries in Wessex. But that is not to say that East Anglia was economically impoverished; indeed quite the contrary; it is just that society was organized rather differently.

There can be little doubt that the population was growing throughout the second and third millennia BC and we see evidence for this in the dividing and sub-dividing of the Fengate Bronze Age landscape. The practice of barrow burial went out of widespread use after about 1400 BC, but it was a very gradual process and anyway barrows had not been used by all classes of society; poor people had always been buried less formally (see 45). Precisely what replaced barrow burial has been a moot point in archaeological circles, but I am in no doubt that the bodies of the more privileged members of society were disposed of in a variety of ways, each accompanied by appropriate ceremonial.

In some cases the method of disposal would be by cremation; indeed, a Bronze Age cremation cemetery and the remains of a large funeral pyre were found by Wyman Abbott at Fengate before the Second World War. Another method involved exposure of the body to the crows on platforms (a rather grisly process known as excarnation). Once the physical bodies had been disposed of, the person's life and spirit were then celebrated, perhaps at an annual gathering.

Later barrow burial is often quite perfunctory: a few cremations in urns let into the edges of earlier barrows, and there seems to be less emphasis on the elaborate disposal of the body. But as the population grew and competition for social prestige rose with it, perhaps people wanted to display their wealth and status not only at death, but also in life, when they needed to impress others and make what in effect was a political statement. This is what we are beginning to see happen between 1400 and 1300 BC when we find the first elaborate metalwork being deliberately thrown into the waters of Fenland. But I am sure that there was also more to it than that. Much of the metalwork we have found at Fengate and Flag Fen was small and insignificant: items such as pins, brooches and razors – what lies behind their deposition? These are some of the questions I will examine in the next chapter.

I would suggest that in our area, if not elsewhere, the far-reaching social changes of the Bronze Age were internally generated: the field and drove system continued in use without modification and when it was finally abandoned, around 1000 BC, the ceremonial site that followed it – a massive row of posts – still respected the same orientation of the landscape. We do not here have evidence for the imposition of new ideas wholesale from outside.

So to summarize, the evidence suggests a rather remote ruling class exerted its influence on the Fengate peasantry at the close of the Neolithic, around 2000 BC. Then as the centuries passed, the old elite became less distantly separated from the population, but at the same time the society of the peasant farmers was also developing, with their own successful and competing families who soon merged with or replaced the old elite. There was then a period between about 2000 and 1300 BC of stability, population growth and social development, culminating around 1000 BC in changes of far-reaching consequence that involved a new pattern of settlement in which people lived more closely with one another in what were in effect embryonic villages and, latterly, towns.

So to return to our original question, what was running through the farmer's mind as he drove his animals down the drove? It depends, of course, on when he drove them, but I suspect that earlier in the Bronze Age he would have been more contented with his lot. Latterly I can imagine he worried a great deal about some competing 'upstart' who was disturbing the even tenor of his otherwise tranquil life. But in both instances he was prosperous and, so far as we can tell, happy enough. Life may have been short, but I can find no reason to suppose it to have been nasty or brutish.

5
The later Bronze Age
(1000-700 BC)

The extraordinary sites at Flag Fen were in effect discovered twice, in 1982 (the Flag Fen platform) and 1989 (the Fengate power station alignment of posts). We now realize that both sites are part of the same complex, but it would be simpler if we considered the two discoveries separately.

The discovery of deeply buried sites

Like many important archaeological discoveries, Flag Fen was found through a combination of luck and opportunism. I am not entirely sure I believe in luck, as it has been observed that lucky archaeologists are simply people who are prepared to spend time and effort finding nothing. True, we found Flag Fen, but nobody hears about the miles of empty dykes we had to look along before we made the big discovery.

Towards the end of chapter 2, I described how and why we decided to look along freshly machine-cleaned drainage dykes. The idea appealed to English Heritage and they agreed to fund a first season of our new Dyke Survey, starting in the autumn of 1982.

Surveying dykes is very hard work. It involves carrying all sorts of equipment (camera and lenses, theodolite, tripod and levelling staff, two range poles, sample bags, finds bags, spade, trowels, notebooks and food for the day), often over very long distances and through heavy clay fields. Much of the time one is walking actually along the dykeside, at an angle of forty-five degrees, and ankles begin to creak under the strain. Clay builds up on the boots to give an effect we call 'moonboots'. Sometimes the dykesides are very simple to interpret and may consist of just one single thick deposit of marine silt. In other cases they can be very complex and require much head-

scratching to sort out (46). The most exciting dykes reveal buried Fen islands whose whole existence was previously unsuspected. In these cases we frequently find evidence that prehistoric groups actually lived around their fringes, just above the water level (47).

We began work by walking along dykes to the east of Peterborough, around the village of Eye. The landscape was flat and highly drained and we found little of immediate archaeological interest, other than huge areas of buried and preserved ancient topsoil. This may not sound particularly exciting to anyone other than an earthworm, but in reality soil science is one of archaeology's major allies. Indeed, if I were to be placed on a desert island, with instructions to work out its ancient history, a soil scientist with archaeological experience would be my right-hand man.

Anyone working in Fenland should have at least a basic knowledge of soils and their recognition, but there are also many occasions when rather more is required, and in these situations I call on the services of our resident archaeological soil scientist, who has been working with me for fifteen years, on and off. Our association started in 1974, when I was directing the Fengate project, ultimately from Toronto. In those early days I was still building up my team, when a young Canadian named Charles French approached me for work. He had just gained a degree in archaeology from Cardiff and had a strong interest in archaeological soil science. I could not believe my luck.

We worked together at Fengate with great success and Charles decided, with the full backing of friends and colleagues, to go for a post-graduate degree at the Institute of Archaeology in London. After a brief return to Canada

46 *Fenland dyke survey. A view along a freshly machine-cleaned dyke, showing the various buried horizons.*

to pick up additional scientific qualifications, Charles started his research in London whilst working for the Fengate project in Peterborough.

Charles French analysed the soils that filled Bronze and Iron Age ditches in Fengate and was able to plot the gradual wettening of the region through a detailed study of the tiny snails preserved in the ground. Snails and other molluscs are often very fussy about where they choose to live and one can reconstruct the surroundings of ancient, long-dead, molluscs if one has detailed knowledge about the residential requirements of their modern descendants. At least that is the theory. In practice it is slightly more complex. Snail shells, especially those of the smaller species do not survive long in the soil if it is at all acid, and that is a big disadvantage of the technique; on the other hand, pollen rarely survives in chalky, non-acid soils, so one can analyse molluscs in situations where one cannot examine pollen. Fengate was just such a situation: it was too dry and chalky to allow the preservation of pollen, but snail shells survived excellently.

As Charles French's research developed he soon realized that snails on their own were not enough, so he broadened his scope to include an even more daunting and informative approach: soil micromorphology. This technique relies on the fact that soil particles carry their history not only in their composition, what they are chemically and physically, but also in the way they sit, or are arranged, in the soil. The technique is to take a brick-sized block of soil, impregnate it with a hard resin, then cut it into thin slices which are ground down so thinly that they become translucent. These slides are then examined under a powerful microscope, using polarized light.

Soil micromorphology can detect episodes of flooding, forest clearance, permanent pasture, ploughing and burning. It also tells one when a soil has been truncated, for example by turf-cutting or water erosion. Indeed, we have been

75

able to demonstrate turf-cutting in buried soils below barrow mounds 4000 years ago.

Normally most archaeological soil scientists are only able to work on ancient soils – *palaeosols* to give them their proper name – in those rare instances where they have been preserved beneath something else, such as a barrow mound or hillfort rampart. In fact I have heard the excavation of an otherwise unthreatened barrow being justified simply because it would allow soil scientists to sample an intact palaeosol. Since the Dyke Survey started in 1982, however, we have demonstrated that there are probably thousands of acres of buried ancient soil out in the Fens, but in these cases the burial was done by the sea or rivers, and not by man. Although less spectacular than Flag Fen, I would rate this discovery as of equal archaeological significance. Study of these huge tracts of palaeosol will give us important and as yet unpredictable new information on the relationship of people to their changing environment, throughout later prehistory. The study will take time and money, but it will be worth every minute and every penny spent. Let

us take an example of what could be achieved.

Archaeologists often try to reconstruct maps of ancient soils using modern soil maps when they are attempting to study the prehistoric economy of a given region. But modern soil maps can only record the top few centimetres of soil – which is visible to the map-maker. Usually this reflects the activities of medieval and modern farmers, industry and so on; anything buried beneath recent river-borne clays is masked from view – and this includes most of the important prehistoric material. In short, modern soil maps simply cannot be used to reconstruct ancient patterns of land use with any real precision. They may be a useful general guide, but no more. In the Fens, on the other hand, Dr French is convinced it will one day be possible to draw *accurate* maps of buried soils of up to five thousand years ago. It is

47 *A typical long Fen dyke. The figure is standing on the prehistoric topsoil of a buried Fen island, the surface of which gradually slopes downwards.*

48 *Starting to split an oak tree in half. Bark is removed to reveal the grain and thin oak wedges are gently hammered in. No slot needs to be cut: the sharp wedge of seasoned oak will penetrate freshly-felled oak.*

almost as if one could take a walk across the ancient countryside, notebook and camera in hand. That is why we were so excited about the buried palaeosols around Eye.

The discovery of Flag Fen

The discoveries at Eye focused our attention on buried soils, and we became rather expert at spotting them, so much so that we were in danger of becoming blinkered to other things. The Dyke Survey operated by finding out from the various drainage authorities precisely where they were planning to dredge or enlarge dykes; we could then select which ones to examine. But the early 1980s were still years of agricultural prosperity and many farmers chose to enlarge their own dykes themselves, and these were best spotted from a Land Rover

which I drove around speculatively. One day I was turning off the River Nene embankment near Northey when, looking across the drained fen 'bay' towards Fengate, I saw the jib of a dragline (a crane-like mechanical digger) in the middle of Flag Fen.

I had done my homework with the drainage authorities, I thought, very thoroughly, and I was surprised to see a big digger in a spot I had always been interested in. The next day I found an excuse to trudge the short distance along the dyke to the digger and asked the driver for whom he was working. It turned out that that particular dyke belonged to the sewage division of the then Anglian Water Authority who were based at the picturesquely-named Crabmarsh in Wisbech.

The gentleman in charge at Crabmarsh, Mr Beel, was extremely helpful and told us to do whatever we liked, provided we did not impede the dyke and flood eastern Peterborough.

For the next two weeks we worked along the cleaned dykeside behind the Anglian Water digger and found a variety of archaeological excitements, including more and more buried

49 *Richard Darrah splitting a halved tree into radial quarters.*

soil. About half-way along its course the dyke cut through a known Roman road, the Fen Causeway, which ran from the town of *Durobrivae*, west of Peterborough, to Fengate, Whittlesey, March and Denver on the Norfolk fen-edge (see **1**). I had excavated a trench across the road at Fengate in 1974, but that was on dry land and I was now keen to see how the Roman military engineers had tackled the wetlands proper. At this point we slowed down and began to examine the dykeside with minute care.

The dyke we were working in is shown on drainage maps as the 'Padholme Engine Drain'. An engine drain in Fen terminology is a dyke leading to a pumping engine – in this case the Padholme Pumping Station that lifts water from the Engine Drain into the River Nene. But being awkward archaeologists we prefer to use the dyke's medieval name of 'Mustdyke'.

The dragline was digging out the bottom of Mustdyke, but the sides were barely touched;

in some respects this was worse than useless as the grass was scuffed up by the bucket and great gobbets of slimy muck made the going somewhat hazardous. So we had to clean the Roman road section with spades, a process that took at least a day. The following day we drew and photographed what we had exposed; the day after that we put the finishing touches on the drawings, but as the weather of late November was now very cold and raw, I decided to pack up and take an early lunch in the warm. I was walking along the top of the dyke, when my foot caught against a piece of wood which almost tripped me up and into the slime. Once I had recovered my composure I was surprised at this event, since there were no trees in the region and bog oak was relatively rare here. So I pulled the wood out of the mud and was even more surprised to see that it had been split across the grain *tangentially*. This rather unusual type of split will require some explanation, and the introduction of yet another key

50 *Starting a tangential split at the end-grain.*

member of our team.

Had I found that piece of wood six months previously I doubt whether I would have recognized its significance. The reason for this is that archaeology was (and still is at many universities) traditionally taught as a dryland subject: students learn about bronzes, pottery, animal and human bones, flint and stone tools (all things that survive in dry conditions), but rarely, if ever, about timber or woodworking. I had picked up a certain amount of knowledge by trawling the academic literature, but there is never any substitute for hands-on experience: I had made pots and knapped flints, but never handled ancient or modern timber, other than to assemble the occasional bookcase. So I decided to do something about it.

In 1976 I employed a student at Fengate who was then doing her degree at the Institute of Archaeology in London. While reading for her degree Maisie Taylor developed an interest in prehistoric woodworking and managed to find courses in wood identification. So she asked me whether I had any ancient timber that needed working on. As it happened, we had just

discovered an early Iron Age well at Fengate which contained a small oak stake that carried a carefully-cut dovetail joint. This fired Maisie's enthusiasm, but there was little else for her to look at, other than a few rather scrappy flecks of charcoal.

As we had little to interest her at Fengate, Maisie turned her attention to Holland where there are many waterlogged sites, rich in timber. She would regularly travel to Amsterdam to work on a site at Assendelft that had been excavated by the Institute of Prehistory, and one day in the autumn of 1982 I persuaded her that she needed an assistant to do things like heavy lifting. Many of the Assendelft timbers were in fact heavy baulks of oak, so I was not altogether surplus to requirements, but while we worked she taught me how to identify the various types of splitting. Incidentally, the reason why people split wood in the Bronze

51 *Making a thin tangentially-split oak plank. This requires a very straight-grained tree and great control.*

Age was quite simply that they did not possess saws; bronze axes were used to cut across the grain, but trees were divided along their length by splitting, using wooden wedges. We have done a certain amount of experimental woodworking at Flag Fen and were taught by Richard Darrah who has an immense amount of practical and theoretical experience of ancient woodworking; frankly we could not have managed without his help and encouragement.

There are two principal ways of splitting a tree, but both methods require the trunk to be split in half initially. When we first did this I simply did not believe that Richard would be able to knock his thin, wooden wedges into oak, without first cutting a small slot (48). However, he very gently started to tap his wedge and as the seasoned oak bit into the softer, freshly-felled 'green' oak, it began to penetrate, at first slowly then with greater rapidity. Wedges were hammered in from both sides and within an hour or so we had split our first oak tree trunk in half.

Having split a tree in half, the next stage is to split the half into quarters (49) and then the quarters into eighths and so on, until one has achieved the size required. This, known as a *radial* split, is by far the easiest type to do, but the resulting timbers are necessarily wedge-shaped, so it is often quite wasteful of wood, as the narrow portion is often removed and discarded.

Parallel-sided planks are far less wasteful of timber and can be produced by splitting across the grain, *tangentially*. It is a far more difficult process than radial splitting and the trick is to place small, sharp, seasoned oak wedges with very great precision in the *end-grain* (not the sides) and to work only with the very best, straight-grained timber (50 and 51). Even then it takes much skill and good luck to achieve a successful result, particularly when one is working in the middle of a forest, miles from anywhere and on a tree that has fallen into a thick layer of soil and leaf-mould that has half buried the trunk (52).

Thus at the Mustdyke on a cold November day in 1982 I was able to recognize that the piece of wood I pulled from the mud had been split across the grain, tangentially. I slid down the side of the dyke to see where it had been dredged from, and caught my foot against a small vertical post that protruded through the grass a few feet above the water. The little post

52 *Woodworking in the depths of the forest. It is probable that trees were split into convenient-sized baulks of timber for transport through the tangled undergrowth.*

was easily pulled from the ground and I was able to identify it as oak (not, I should add, a particularly difficult feat). I was immediately struck by the fact that the post weighed almost nothing, yet oak is usually very dense; I was also struck by the fact that the tip had been sharpened all round, pencil-fashion, by an axe with a very narrow, curved blade – no more than about 40 mm (1½ in.) wide.

Many Fen dykes have posts in their sides to reinforce areas of loose peat or of 'running silts' (old stream courses that are still partially active). I knew, however, that this particular dyke was fairly stable, and besides, modern posts are usually of pine or spruce, chemically-treated, and invariably saw-sharpened. I hung

53 *Flag Fen in the early days: access was by boat.*

my coat on a pole I put in to mark the post and chopped into the dykeside with my trowel. No sooner had I started to clear the grass than I found small pieces of wood protruding from the dykeside, slightly less than a metre ($3\frac{1}{4}$ ft) above the post. There was something about the regularity of their arrangement that made me think that they had been put there by the hand of man, perhaps as part of a track or something of the sort. Then I happened to look along the dykeside, back towards the Roman road whose orange gravel make-up seemed to glow in the distance, and I tingled as I realized that the timbers I had been prodding with my trowel were about 1 m ($3\frac{1}{4}$ ft) below the bottom of the Roman road. On the assumption that the peats thereabouts accumulated at the rate of about a millimetre (0.04 in.) a year, then there was every chance that the post and the smaller timbers dated to about 1000 BC. I then retrieved a camera from my coat pocket and recorded

the scene for posterity (**colour plate 3**).

After lunch I decided not to return to the dyke, as it was latish in November, the light was failing, and freezing fog was rolling in from the Wash. So I drove home, tired but happy. We could not get back to the dyke for a couple of days, the weather being so bad, but when we did, it was with a team of six people (**53**). By now we were equipped with spades and were prepared to use them. When we reached the spot where I had left the marker pole I resumed trowelling where I had left off, fully expecting, if it was indeed a trackway, to come to its edges before too long. But I did not. Then, about 18 m (60 ft) to my right, Charles French gave a shout and we all rushed over to see what he had found: it was a 15 cm (6 in.) wide tangentially split oak plank with other oak pieces around it. So we enlarged our makeshift excavation on either side of this new find (**54**). A few moments later David Gurney hit another plank, but this time it had a mortice hole through which a peg had been driven; this was important as it showed that the wood was still in place (**55**). Then there was another cry from Dave

54 *Flag Fen: after three days' excavation, wood is appearing in some quantity.*

Crowther, who was an improbable 27 m (90 ft) away and he had found more planks. I looked around and the two people on either side of my original find were about 36 m (120 ft) apart. None of us believed for a moment that we were revealing parts of the same site.

We broke for lunch in a state of great over-excitement, hurried our food and returned to the fray. Everywhere we looked we seemed to find ancient timber. By the end of the day the dykeside looked as if a bomb had hit it, and looking back as we headed home we decided it was time we behaved like archaeologists. So the next day we tidied up the loose earth and began to excavate a step-like trench along the dykeside, in the hope that at some point the wood would cease (**56**).

Although quite dry, being so close to the edge of the dyke, some of the wood was still remarkably well preserved and one piece in particular seems to have been used as a carpen-

ter's chopping-block as it carried the distinct tool-marks of some six separate implements, mainly axes and chisels (**57**).

Flag Fen: discovering the size of the site
After three days' work it was apparent to anyone that we had found something of major importance and I decided to find out who actually owned it. So I left the two Daves and Charles French digging, while Maisie rushed from one to another examining the wood, and headed for Anglian Water in Wisbech. Mr Beel heard me out and then said he had a small confession to make. It would appear that Anglian Water had last deepened and enlarged that dyke in 1976 and he was the Resident Engineer on the job. He remembered the spot well, because their mechanical digger had actually been brought to a standstill by vast amounts of timber, which they had thought – quite reasonably – were the remains of a Victorian sluice. As I recall, I said that if that was a typical example of his artefact-dating, I would make a better engineer than he would an archaeologist.

55 *The first evidence that some of the horizontal wood is* in situ. *This oak plank has been secured into the ground with a peg through the mortice hole.*

Mr Beel then set about helping us in every way possible: we were given a boat and a secure place to work from, and we learned that the land to one side of the dyke belonged to the Anglian Water Authority who used it to spread and dispose of Peterborough's sewage sludge. We had certainly noticed a slight heaviness in the air. I was then put in touch with the AWA's estates people with whom we negotiated access rights.

Meanwhile the team in the dyke were still digging away, with no sign of an end in sight. Eventually, after about two weeks' work the wood ceased to appear, but not before we had excavated, planned, photographed and exposed

over 80 m (260 ft) of timber along the dykeside (**58**). Next we had to sample and remove about 500 pieces which were threatened with immediate destruction now that they were exposed to the air. We did this by boat until in the second week of December the weather clamped down, and then we used the Anglian Water Authority's tough little double-hulled fibreglass boat as a sledge on the frozen water. The last pieces of wood were prised from the ground by frozen fingers on Christmas Eve. By this time most of the team had returned to their families for the festivities and I well remember the strange feeling when, as Maisie and I hauled the last boatload of wood along the dyke and it began to snow lightly, we realized that Peterborough had gone silent for the holiday. By nine o'clock the normal roar of traffic had ceased and for a few moments, trudging through the mud in the middle of nowhere, we felt more in touch with

56 By early December 1982 it soon became apparent that the wood had been placed in the ground in a deliberate, if rough, criss-cross pattern.

the remote past than with our own time.

After Christmas we were visited by Dr Geoffrey Wainwright, now Chief Archaeologist of English Heritage and in those days the Principal Inspector for rescue archaeology. By this time there had been much media attention and I felt somewhat uneasy, as I knew he could be very sceptical and was used to the over-enthusiasm of colleagues. We walked along the dykeside on a fine January morning and then suddenly a grass snake slithered out of the mud in front of us, shimmered down the bank and entered the water without a ripple. We were both delighted and the mood then became very positive. I hope that snake lived happily, had a large family – and died of a surfeit of frogs.

Geoffrey Wainwright put his finger on our problem: we had over 80 m (260 ft) of prehistoric timber, representing a vast amount of labour,

and yet we had not found anything else – no pots, flints or bronzes. It seemed to be important, but what was it? He was reluctant to commit large sums of money to a site of unknown size or purpose, which, in retrospect, is reasonable enough – although at the time, of course, I felt we should be given carte blanche to do anything we chose, regardless of expense. We were told we could spend £4000 to discover (a) what it (Flag Fen) was and (b) its size. A challenge, I thought – and with some justification.

The next year was frantically busy, but not at Flag Fen: our main site in 1983 was a waterlogged Neolithic ceremonial site near Maxey, in the Welland valley, just north of Peterborough. The quarry next to this site had turned its huge pumps on and we were digging flat-out to recover everything we could before

57 An oak spar was found that had been used as a carpenter's chopping block, as demonstrated by the tool-marks.

58 *The dyke at the end of the first season, 1982, with wood extending continuously along the dykeside.*

it was all sucked dry. It was hard work, but worth it. It produced an extraordinary amount of material, including a wooden Neolithic axe-handle and the earliest piece of fine string yet found in England, both of which are on display in the British Museum. By the end of the summer we all needed a rest, but instead we started at Flag Fen; at the time I felt it should be renamed Flagging Fen.

It had been a very hot season and when we returned to the Mustdyke we were shocked by the state of things (**59**). The dyke was almost dry and the few pieces of Bronze Age wood were twisted, cracked and worthless. We could not dig away from the dykeside, as the land was occupied by a fine field of standing wheat. So, after looking around, we decided to place a trench on the dykeside in an area of upright posts (**60**). We had spent a couple of days digging there, when combine harvesters arrived and

the wheat was duly harvested. Next day the straw and stubble were fired and we were given three days to complete a borehole survey, before the tractors returned to sow the next season's crop. In those days land in East Anglia did not spend much time lying fallow. The weather stayed hot and dry and then winds began to blow. In the gales peat was blown off the land around the site and swiftly fell to earth in the relatively still air of the dyke (**61**). Sometimes we would return in the morning to find a thick layer of wind-sorted dry peat covering the wood we had spent the previous day uncovering. It could be quite frustrating.

Charles French and I rapidly laid out a 20 m (66 ft) grid over the field's surface and we started to drill boreholes. It was backbreaking work, especially pulling the drill out against the vacuum caused by damp peat, but it was worth the pain. After three days we had a fairly clear picture: wood, and much of it oak or ash which could not have grown in the peat and must therefore have been brought in from outside, extended over an area of about 0.8 ha (2 acres). The site was far larger than we had ever imagined. Then the tractors rolled onto the field and we returned to the dykeside trench amongst the uprights.

We soon found the tops of posts, many of which were oak, and worked our way down alongside them. About 60 cm (2 ft) below their tops (which had rotted-off at some time in the distant past) we came across horizontal timbers. These were removed to reveal smaller pieces, including many chips which strongly suggested that an axe had actually been used *in situ*. The woodchips rested in a mixture of peaty mud and a very distinct coarse white sand with fine gravel pebbles which Charles French said could not have been washed there by water, as the stones were too large and heavy. This was all very intriguing, but we had still not answered Geoffrey Wainwright's first, and most important, question: what was it?

About a week into the excavation Charles French found five pieces of coarse, hand-made

pottery from the same vessel. I took one look and was in no doubt at all that it was of Late Bronze Age date. Quite simply it was too horrible to be anything else (**62**). Southern English Late Bronze Age pottery is rarely decorated and often seems to have been made by folk who took a delight in doing things badly; the pieces before us were no exception, and had the look and texture of wet wholemeal biscuit. This texture is often caused by the dissolving-out of fossil shell originally ground up and added to the clay as a tempering agent; this allowed a cooking-pot to accept repeated heating without cracking. We will see below that Bronze Age pottery can be very fine, but this is the exception, rather than the rule.

A few months previously the British Museum Research Laboratory had rushed us through a radiocarbon date that placed the dykeside timber in the Late Bronze Age, just after 1000 BC. Those few sherds of pottery were all-important, as they provided independent confirmation of the date. The form of the vessel, a simple jar, suggested that it had a domestic or household purpose. Of course it could have

59 *The same view as* **58**, *10 months later, after a hot, dry summer*

60 *Damage caused by the summer weather.*

been thrown into Flag Fen from a boat, together with the general household rubbish, but the usual practice in pre-Roman Britain was to dispose of refuse near the spot where it was produced. It was rarely transported any distance, and as the closest dry land was at least 200 m (660 ft) away, it seemed reasonable to suppose that people might have been living, or camping, nearby in the wetland.

The results of the 1983 survey and excavation were sufficiently encouraging for English Heritage to give us a proper excavation grant for the season of 1984. By now we had established excellent relations with the water authorities who agreed to retain the dyke water at a higher level in an effort to slow down the drying-out. Flag Fen had also been recently visited by

Professor Louwe-Kooijmans of Leiden University in the Netherlands. The professor has extensive experience of de-watered peat sites and was of the opinion that the timbers of Flag Fen would be seriously decayed within fifteen to twenty years, unless something was done to slow down desiccation. At the time there was no alternative but to excavate, since the only solution, as we then thought, was to flood the whole of Flag Fen and with it the farms and houses of many of its modern inhabitants. Since then we have constructed the artificial lake and are learning how to impede drainage generally.

We decided in 1984 to enlarge the previous season's small trench around the posts, and to concentrate our efforts along the edge of the dyke, because that was where drying-out was most severe. The upper soil had been compacted into an almost solid mass by the heavy machines used to dredge the dyke in 1976 and

1982, and we simply could not remove it by hand. So I decided to call in a machine of our own to clear a reasonably-sized area, but before I did so I determined to carry out a search of the topsoil surface before we disturbed it with our excavations and spoil heaps.

We did not expect to find anything very ancient in the topsoil, as the Bronze Age levels were all deeply buried, but in the material that had been dredged out of the dyke we found about half a dozen human bones, which we assumed, for no reason at all, were the remains of medieval fishermen. In 1989 we found another two loose human bones, again alongside the Mustdyke, on the surface. We will discuss the significance of these discoveries at the end of this chapter.

After our machine had removed the tough upper crust, we removed the remaining overburden by hand. We placed our trench alongside the dyke and made it just 5 m (16½ ft) wide and 10 m (33 ft) long, although it grew in length

as time progressed. As we came down on the tops of the posts it was quite apparent that they were arranged in four somewhat irregular rows. We continued downwards, below the post tops and encountered the first horizontal wood. As in the previous year, the highest horizontal wood was unvariably unsplit ('roundwood' to give its correct name) and was more spread-out and less cluttered than the timber below.

We left the highest timber in place, as we could work around it, and continued down. The next layer was also rather irregular and consisted mainly of roundwood too, but individual pieces were generally smaller. Below this was the layer of small woodchips and coarse white sand that we had come across the previous season and in which we had found the five fragments of pottery. By now we were becoming swamped with wood, so we removed the upper two layers, to expose the layer of chips and sand below them. This layer was very much flatter than the previous two and had a clearly defined surface. We also gained the impression that it was thicker in places where it had been laid over hollows; in many parts

61 *'Fen blow' deposits peat in the dyke.*

62 *Five pieces of Late Bronze Age pottery, broken in antiquity; the first non-wooden items found at Flag Fen. They were found in a thin layer of sand and gravel around the posts.*

63 *Flag Fen, 1984–86. Plan of the upright timbers, forming the probable wall and roof-support timbers of a three-aisled building. (After PPS 1986.)*

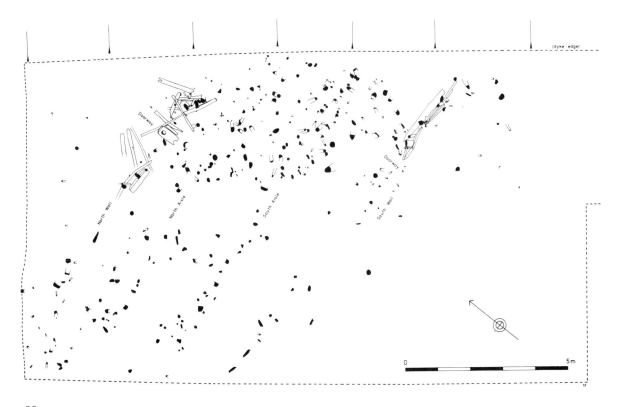

64 *Starting work on the enlarged dykeside excavation, 1984. The highest layer of horizontal wood is being exposed.*

there were also clear indications that planks or small boards had been laid down as a support or reinforcement beneath. Rather to our relief we also found more archaeological artefacts in amongst the sand and woodchips: several dozen sherds of coarse Bronze Age pottery, some very crudely fashioned flint implements and a fossil echinoid, or sea urchin, about the size of a tennis ball, which I stoutly maintain (but cannot demonstrate) was a child's toy. The layer of sand, woodchips and pottery was only found within the area occupied by the vertical posts; it was not found anywhere else.

Flag Fen was quite unlike any other site we had excavated until that point, and its interpretation was clearly going to cause us difficulties. At first glance one might assume that because we had so much information, and so very well preserved, that understanding its significance would be relatively straightforward. That is not always the case however. In my experience, the more archaeological information you possess, the more (and not the less) there is to explain. Poorly preserved archaeological evidence seems easy to interpret and can be very convincing to everyone – except those who have actually had to wrestle with well-preserved complex sites themselves.

This 'uncertainty principle' applies to Fengate and Flag Fen: the very first, early Neolithic landscape (chapter 3) is just hinted-at by a few aligned ditches and mortuary structures, and yet it is quite convincing. Flag Fen, on the other hand, is superbly preserved, but there are still huge problems that cannot be resolved, because the wealth of evidence is always providing good reasons to reject any promising new ideas.

Flag Fen: interpretations emerge

It was clear that the sand and woodchip layer at Flag Fen was more-or-less *in situ*. It was also clear that it was closely related to the posts, as it did not occur away from them. The posts were carefully mapped onto large-scale plans, and it was immediately apparent that they formed four distinct rows (**63**). The rows, moreover, were plainly parallel and this suggested that they ought either to be contemporary with each other, or to have been part of a single structure that was repaired and renewed over time. After much head-scratching we decided that we were excavating the remains of a rectangular building, of as yet unknown length, constructed on a large timber platform in the middle of the fen. The width of the building, 6 m (19 ft) was closely comparable with an almost contemporary one at the site of Assendelft in Holland, as were the other dimensions of its three-aisled construction. Moreover, coarse white sand is frequently found on the floors of 'crannogs' (fortified farmsteads on artificial islands in lakes) in Scotland and Ireland, to prevent feet sliding about.

This hypothesis made, and still makes, sense: it explains the presence of broken household pottery, of animal bones and flint tools. But there are drawbacks, principally the plethora of posts, which as we will see below, can now be explained. The upper two layers, if such they be, represent collapsed timber from roof and walls.

The following season, 1985, we continued in the same trench and were beginning to develop excavation techniques that were suited to a site that had no edges or 'safe' areas where one could kneel and work, once, that is, one had removed the overlying peat (**64**). The previous season we had encased the trench in scaffolding which simply rested on the ground, except along the dykeside where it was safe to drive in posts (since all archaeological remains had long since dried out). This framework had to

65 *General view of the excavations from across the Mustdyke.*

66 *The sprinkler system in operation.*

break all the accepted rules of scaffolding, but it worked and was stable (**65**). We used it to divide the trench up into smaller areas and it provided a means of fixing suspended platforms above the wood, from which people could work.

Sunlight and wind tended to dry the wood, so we erected a plastic-covered shelter over the dig, using the scaffold frame as a foundation, but this was never very satisfactory and after windy nights we would often return to the site to find ropes snapped, eyelets ripped out and the sheets in tatters. In 1984 we kept the site wet with relays of watering cans, but this again was not altogether satisfactory, and in 1985 we replaced cans with an aged agricultural sprinkling system which usually worked but which we found less than endearing when the

ancient tractor's battery failed, or the fuel lines blocked up (**66**).

In our excavations on dry sites we had often used sieves of various sorts as a means of trying to standardize methods of finding things. In theory (although not, I suspect, in practice) archaeological sieves are meant to remove the bias in finds distribution caused by sharp-eyed versus myopic excavators. At Flag Fen we found that sieves of all types simply clogged-up with wood and peat; we still try to use them, however, but more in hope, than for any practical benefit.

In 1986 we acquired a more robust type of industrial shelter from a friendly and helpful firm in Bedford and today we use the same firm's large plastic-covered temporary warehouse to shelter the dig (**67**). This extraordinary building stood through the 1987 hurricane in southern England and is built in Sweden to their very

67 *Erecting the steel frame of the new excavation shelter.*

68 *Planning the wood using conventional manual techniques. The planner (left) leans over a drawing board and views the wood below through a gridded frame.*

demanding Building Regulations. We no longer blanket the site in scaffolding, as we found that it often collapsed, especially when wet, and excavators complained of headaches and pop-eyes after spending six hours hanging off a suspended platform. Now we use strips of discarded industrial floor-covering material to spread people's weight, and it seems to work quite effectively.

We used to draw maps of the wood by balancing on the scaffolding and looking down through a small gridded-frame (68). We realized the limitations of this method and so we also made a somewhat crude photo-montage of the wood using a specially adapted surveyor's tripod. Charles French was the ace-planner, using this technique, but we now use a more sophisticated system, based on a monorail-mounted camera that travels around a U-shaped rail in the roof of the warehouse structure. This produces an accurate photo-montage of the site which we then trace to make our working plans. It also provides us with spectacular bird's eye views (**colour plate 4**). In the future we plan to computerize the whole photographic planning operation, but it will always require an archaeologist, on the ground, to decide what is significant and what can be rejected.

The winter of 1984/85 was quite severe and we had bedded the site below a 'sandwich' of straw between two layers of plastic sheeting. In theory it was a splendid idea, but when it came to the task of removing it we found that the large local population of rats had found it an ideal spot in which to nest and raise healthy

69 *Doorway in the north wall. The squat plank with the mortice hole is part of the threshold. The wood is distorted by drying-out.*

70 *Fragment of a Late Bronze Age shale bracelet.*

young families. We have not repeated the experiment. When the covers were eventually cleared away we found that the archaeological layers survived the rodents unscathed, so we resumed work on the sand and chip floor.

We had put forward the building hypothesis and we now sought evidence to prove or disprove it. The two outer rows of posts were taken to be the walls, and in the north wall there was a clear doorway-sized gap. A certain amount of sand and fine gravel had been spread immediately outside the gap, presumably by trampling feet, and at the threshold we found a very large tangentially split oak plank with two mortice holes (**69**); another smaller plank had been jammed between it and the presumed door post and a stout peg had been driven through one of the mortice holes, flush with the surface. Outside this doorway was the 'yard', if we may call it that, of the platform, and it had been additionally consolidated with

oak timber off-cuts and a discarded yoke-like object with two perforations that may now be seen on display in the British Museum.

Only a small part of the 'yard' surface north of the posts was inside the trench, but our excavations in 1985 and 1986 showed it to have been carefully built, with a surface that had been pegged in position in places. One of these pegs had been cut from a coppiced or pollarded tree and given a sharpened tip; the piece at the top was plainly part of the coppice 'bole' and consisted of highly characteristic gnarled, burr wood. In other words, the peg was complete; it could never have extended any higher. When we excavated it, the gnarled top protruded some 7.5 to 10 cm (3–4 in.) above the yard surface it had originally held in place. This demonstrated (a), that the yard surface was *in situ* and (b), that shrinkage caused by drying out was not as severe – a mere 7.5 to 10 cm (3–4 in.) – as we had once feared.

Below the yard surface we were amazed to come across not rough brushwood and scrappy rejects, as we had anticipated, but large baulks of trimmed timber, much of it, moreover, of oak.

Then, in amongst the lowest, largest timbers we found our first really unusual find, a piece from a polished shale bracelet (**70**); normally speaking on dry sites, the shale tends to flake and laminate, but our example was black and shiny. I have seen identical bracelets on my grandmother's dressing-table. We have since found many more, and although the type is relatively common on Late Bronze Age domestic sites, we were still delighted. Besides, I now have good reasons to suppose that these shale bracelets were deliberately broken and were anything but domestic items.

The posts of the building's south wall (**71**) also had a gap, but it was slightly staggered from that with the threshold plank on the north

71 *View of the south wall showing the cavity construction on either side of the main wall and supporting posts (metre scale).*

side – an arrangement that would help to prevent through-draughts. The south wall doorway was paved with a thick layer of woodchips and again, the yard surface outside showed signs of trample and had been pegged down in many places. The doorpost was a stump with a protruding peg which originally fitted into a socket in the door (**72**). A similar arrangement is known from a prehistoric door in Switzerland, only there it is the other way around: the peg is integral with the door and swivels in a socket in the floor. The Flag Fen arrangement would seem more efficient, as the socket would remain free of sand and other grinding agents. The 'shoulder' of the Flag Fen door swivel post was 7.5–10 cm (3–4 in.) above the surrounding floor level, confirming the shrinkage we had estimated from the coppiced peg of the north yard surface.

We next turned our attention to the outside

72 *A possible door pivot post in the south (outer) wall (scale in cms).*

walls. The south wall east of the doorway was the best preserved, and here we found the very base of the wall which consisted of two planks, one on the inside and one on the outside of the building, which were pegged against the main roof-support posts. These carried the weight of the wall cladding and would be termed by architects a 'sill-plate'. The wall cladding consisted of long rods, about 5 cm (2 in.) in diameter which were pegged against the posts by vertical pegs driven into the peat. This gave, in effect, a cavity wall slightly less than 50 cm (20 in.) thick. The surrounding peaty alluvium would have made an excellent 'daub', but it is difficult to say with any confidence whether or not it

was used to coat the walls (72).

Below the floor layer, or layers, the foundations consisted of many large timbers which were clearly intended to carry a substantial load (73). Some of the wall and roof-support posts had collapsed, and one had come down on a near-complete pot. Maisie Taylor has identified many samples of wood and has shown that oak was almost invariably split or modified in some way and was most commonly used in and around the building. Ash was a less important building timber, and was frequently split into halves. Rather surprisingly, the types of wood that grow most readily in the fen, namely willow, sallow and poplar were used infrequently, with the important exception of alder (see 80), which is probably the single most commonly found species of tree at Flag Fen. When kept wet it resists rot well, but is otherwise a poor timber for construction purposes.

73 *The excavation was enlarged in 1985 to reveal the tops of wall posts in a row behind the figure. The lower foundation timbers can be seen in the foreground.*

74 *Late Bronze Age willow scoop* in situ.

Slightly more than 1 m (3¼ ft) outside the south wall was a very wide-spaced row of posts which leaned away from the building. These were probably used to support the broad eaves which kept the mud walls dry. Beyond the eaves-support posts was the southern platform

or 'yard' surface. The south platform area was made up from rather smaller wood than that to the north, but it still included many carpentry off-cuts and a few artefacts, such as a very finely-made willow scoop, which is now on display in the British Museum (**74**).

The edges of the platform

In 1986 we decided to investigate the edge of the platform to the south of the posts, since the dykeside investigation of 1982, had shown it petered out in a rather unconvincing fashion. So we extended the 5m- (16½ft-) wide trench along the dyke and, just as in 1982, the wood kept on going; eventually it ceased to appear. As we had suspected from the outset, instead of petering out, the platform had been carefully edged with a 'boardwalk' about 3.5 m (11 ft) wide made from planks and roundwood arranged circumferentially, parallel with the edge of the platform (not, as we had suspected, radially or spoke-fashion). One of the split oak planks was an extraordinary 3.25 m (10 ft) in length (**75**). There were a few pieces of driftwood beyond the 'boardwalk', but these aside, the contrast between the timber platform and the fen around it was most marked (**76**).

The following season (1987) we investigated the foundations of the boardwalk which had been built upon at least three layers of timber, laid in a rough criss-cross pattern. But perhaps the most interesting discovery came last. The lowest timbers included a very large oak post with a pencil-like sharpened tip. We at once recognized it as an upright that had been pulled from the ground, and there was distinctive yellowy-grey clay still sticking to its tip. This clay had preserved the axe-marks beneath it superbly, and in this particular case the post had actually been sharpened by an axe with two deep notches in its blade, which show up clearly as low ridges in the wood (**77**). Less than a pace away was the hole from which it had been extracted (by pulling, not digging) before being dropped on the ground. There were no other posts in the immediate vicinity, so it is currently difficult to decide whether this massive post stood on its own, or formed part of an encircling defensive palisade.

The story of the edge revetment was resumed in the spring of 1988 when many of our visitors expressed a wish to see something 'fenny', that resembled Bronze Age Flag Fen. The planting of trees, shrubs and marginal reeds around the

lake had yet to grow up, and I decided to make a ramp down to the Mustdyke whose edges were covered with reeds, rushes and sedge; we then planned to build a wooden walkway to the main excavation along the dykdeside 'step' we had excavated in 1982; as a bonus, people on their way to the dig could view the Roman road from under a protective shelter.

The ramp was positioned to one side of the timber, well north of the point where it had petered out in 1982. Needless to state, despite our careful plans to avoid any timbers, we placed the ramp right on top of the platform's northern perimeter. Being at the extreme dyke edge, drying out was quite severe, but we were able to excavate the trunks of several trees, mainly of alder (see **80**), which had been placed on the ground in precisely the same way as the more formal 'boardwalk' at the other side of the platform (**78**). Again, the trunks had been raised on supporting horizontals, but on a generally smaller scale than below the 'boardwalk' on the other side of the platform.

In 1986 we obtained permission to do a borehole survey on the other, east, side of the Mustdyke. This was not made any easier by the Roman road which ran across the area, but we were able to demonstrate that there was wood extending in a large semi-circle from the two extremes in the dykeside about 40 to 50 m (130 to 165 ft) into the field. This additional survey now gave us a fairly good impression of the timber platform's size.

Public archaeology at Flag Fen

The year 1987 was crucially important to Flag Fen. The previous winter Geoffrey Wainwright had secured for us a conditional promise of £475,000 from English Heritage, to be spent over the five years from 1988 to 1992. This sum was subject to strict Treasury limits and could not be stretched, so we decided that now was the time to 'go public' and we opened the site for a trial period of 13 weeks from August to October. I have already mentioned the construction of the lake (chapter 2), and while we were digging down to insert the plastic film, we encountered wood virtually everywhere, which confirmed our fears that the borehole

75 *The platform perimeter was bounded by an arrangement of planks, known as the 'boardwalk'.*

76 *Close-up view of the 'boardwalk'.*

survey had been rather conservative about the extent of the platform. More importantly, we found groups of buried posts at seven different points around the lake's circumference; some of these may have been buildings, others on the other hand, may have had a very different purpose.

It was clear that the public would not be particularly impressed by our dykeside excavations which were nearing completion and were beginning to look rather careworn. So we decided to concentrate our efforts at the northern end of the trench and remove every-

77 *Cut-end of a felled tree; the axe marks were very clear, the axe's cutting-edge had two nicks.*

thing there. Slightly to our surprise we found that none of the posts had been dug into the ground: all carried long pencil-like sharpened tips that had been pile-driven into the clay and gravel that underlies the peat.

When the last posts had been removed, we erected the new Swedish building and the visitor walkway. One wall of the building is 1 m (3¼ ft) taller than the other and stands in the old excavation trench; this keeps damage, caused by the steel stakes that pin the building to the ground, to a minimum. The new shelter allowed us to excavate a larger area, and under almost ideal conditions. By now we were becoming far better organized and tended to work all year round, even excavating well into the winter. Similarly our post-excavation research was going ahead both in the winter, and during the summer months. Excavating 'seasons' were becoming less sharply defined; there was, in effect, continuous work. So we

78 *The platform was revetted on its north side also. In this instance small tree trunks were used instead of planks.*

will treat the discoveries of 1987 to 1989 as a single entity.

Changing interpretations: our latest views

The three types of layer first identified in 1984 were again encountered in the new trench: an upper 'collapse' (**colour plate 5**), then a sandy floor (**colour plate 6**), with foundations below (**colour plate 9**). The timbers of the building continued in four rows, as before, with eaves-support posts on the south side (the north side was outside the excavation). Again, there were numerous examples of morticed planks and other pieces that had been pegged down – one timber was secured by no less than 14 small pegs. There could be no doubt that the floor and lower timbers had been carefully placed into position.

The higher levels produced surprises, too.

Just outside another entranceway in the south wall were several large oak timbers, including a plank with mortice holes at each end and a large, unused post with a characteristic pencil-like tip, which this time was not coated with clay (**colour plate 7**). Its other end, the top, was carefully fashioned into a flat shoulder with a prominent, long tenon (**79**). This post (labelled B61) was probably about to be used to replace an eaves-support, when water levels rose and the small dump of 'builder's supplies' was abandoned outside the building (**80** and **colour plate 8**). Maisie Taylor has suggested very provisionally that the building's super-structure involved quite sophisticated carpentry (**81**).

The 1988 season had an additional surprise in store for us. It was made to one side of our visitors' car-park, in rough grass, where we accidentally came across numerous oak timbers, deeply buried beneath the surface. The tool-marks were identical to the ones we had been looking at for years at Flag Fen, and there was no reason to doubt that this new discovery was part of the Bronze Age timber platform. If

79 *An unused eaves-support post was found lying outside the building; note the pencil-like point.*

these timbers were indeed part of the same platform, then it must be almost a third as large again as we had originally estimated. It was a daunting prospect.

Finds from excavations since 1987 have included large amounts of pottery, another, bigger shale bracelet fragment, a somewhat decayed small bronze dagger with three rivets, a ball-headed bronze stick pin (**colour plate 10**) and many animal bones. At first glance, this collection of material looks ordinary enough, but is it? The pottery, for instance, generally joins together if one makes the effort to restore it, and this is not what one would expect of a 'normal' domestic site. Two of the vessels were found almost complete and one had undoubtedly been deliberately placed in the ground underneath the floor, because a log had been pegged into position above it – and yet the fragile pot was undamaged. Pots may be found on domestic sites, but complete daggers are certainly very unusual.

Most of the finds are straightforwardly Late Bronze Age in appearance, but the complete jar with pinched-up decoration around the belly, and the dagger with three rivets could equally well date to the Middle Bronze Age (**colour plate 10**). To be more precise: the Late Bronze Age finds post-date 1000 BC, while the Middle Bronze ones pre-date it. Only one find is demonstrably post-Bronze Age: a safety-pin-style brooch of the later Iron Age which was found on the south side of the posts, but at a significantly higher level than the Bronze Age items. We once regarded this as an accidental loss: an item mislaid in the water after a pleasant afternoon's picnic in the Fens. It will shortly be plain how wrong we were.

The Power Station sub-site, Fengate

The story begins conventionally enough: we had employed a contractor to dig a trench for the water main which was to service our new visitors' toilets. This main was run from the end of Fourth Drove, along the canalized Cat's Water, along the Roman road and thence to the Visitor Centre. We treated this as an opportunity to put an archaeological trench straight across most of Flag Fen, and so we kept a very

80 *An alder log in the process of being split by a wooden wedge (scale in cms).*
81 *Suggested reconstruction of some of the Flag Fen building's superstructure, using numbered timbers found together on the south side of the structure. The outer wall is represented by timbers B285 and B47; the eaves-support posts are B73 and B31. (Jo Richards.)*

close eye on operations.

As the work progressed, we noted that there were oak posts in the trench where it skirted our car-park; these were heading, it seemed, in the direction of Fengate. Was this the causeway we had hoped to find, linking the Flag Fen timber platform to fen-edge dry land at Fengate? I kept my fingers crossed. A few days later, when the digger had started to work

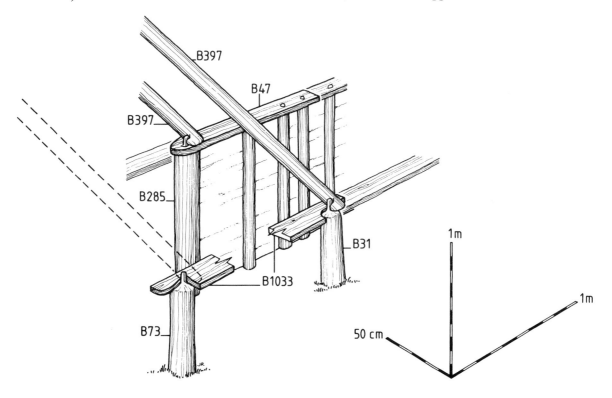

parallel to the Cat's Water dyke we knew that something might well happen – and it did. One day we spotted posts about 200 m (660 ft) west of the Roman road, close to the belt of trees that marks the edge of the New Town.

No sooner had the machine revealed the first few posts than we fitted it with a wide, toothless bucket, and cleared an area about 3 m (10 ft) wide and 20 m (66 ft) long, between the water main and the Cat's Water ditch. There were nearly thirty posts, mostly of split oak, together with a number of oak planks which seemed to be *in situ*. It was all very reminiscent of Flag Fen, but on a much smaller scale; sadly, too, it was very much drier (**82**). Now, it is very hard to make sense of so small a 'keyhole', but the posts were possibly heading towards our car-park and the main Flag Fen excavation beyond. In short it really did seem that we had found the long-lost causeway. We took six samples for radiocarbon dating and sent them to Cambridge University; three were from posts, three from planks near the posts. The results show beyond reasonable doubt that the sampled posts and planks are of the same date, namely, the Late Bronze Age.

Two years later I was approached by the City Planning Department about a power station that it was proposed should be built on the field immediately north and west of the Cat's Water, on land that we dubbed somewhat unoriginally the Power Station sub-site (**83**). This was one of the lowest-lying fields in Fengate and it was plain that our posts, if they were indeed part of a causeway, must run across a large part of it. We put this to the developers, Hawker Siddeley Power Engineering Ltd, who agreed to fund an exploratory excavation.

We started the dig in April 1989 and finished it in October, after the hottest, driest summer on record. To cut a long story short, we found the posts where we had expected, and excavated a long, thin trench to expose them (**84**). They ran in a band about 10 to 12 m (33–40 ft) wide and some 150 m (495 ft) long, from the lowest-lying area, where they were relatively well preserved, to the higher gravel of the Fen-margin proper, where all that was left were just a few brown stains and smears of peat-like powder (**85**).

Before we extended the trench westwards, towards the dry land, we had to decide the level to which we would strip mechanically. The overburden consisted of over 1 m (3¼ ft) of very

82 *The excavation of a narrow trench for a water main revealed a number of posts. The trench was widened and horizontal timbers were also found.*

stiff river-borne clay and hand-digging was impossible; on the other hand, if we went too deep we would damage the posts, particularly their upper portions which, as we will see, were especially important. So we stayed as high as we could, but were aware of the fact that we would only expose a proportion of the actual posts in the alignment (**86**).

As soon as I saw the first few posts exposed I was convinced that our 'causeway' was nothing of the sort, although I still had no idea what it was. In archaeology it is often half the battle if one can quickly rid oneself of a hypothesis that is no longer applicable; in this case the original posts exposed in the water-main trench had been accompanied by planks that seemed to be in their original position *below* the posts. That, on reflection, was not

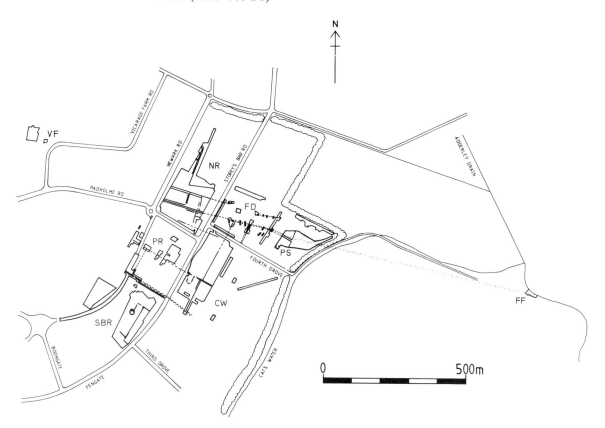

83 *Map showing the relationship of the Fengate Power Station post alignment to the earlier Bronze Age ditched field system and the current Flag Fen excavations (FF). PS = Power Station sub-site. (Martin Redding.)*

what might be expected of a causeway, which must by definition be raised above the wet. Then the radiocarbon dates were also rather odd: they were all virtually contemporary, and yet they were taken from posts across the line; normally one might expect a causeway to be maintained in use for some time and the dates should reflect this. These two observations, plus strong intuitive misgivings, led me to doubt the causeway idea as the only explanation for the posts. I still do not discount it entirely: it is quite possible, indeed probable, that the posts, whatever their purpose, are following the line of an ancient route of some sort.

The machine finished in early summer by which time we had exposed nearly 800 posts of which over 95 per cent were of oak. We then placed hand-cut trenches across the alignment and to nobody's surprise more than doubled the number of posts. We would now estimate that the total number of posts on the Power Station sub-site alone is well over 2000. The new posts that appeared in the hand-cut sections were generally smaller than the others, and this probably explains why they had not survived so high up in the soil. The post alignment on the Power Station field was wider, by about 2–3 m (6½–9½ ft) than at Flag Fen, and the posts were generally smaller, but there were clear signs of rather wobbly rows.

At this point in the excavation it became apparent that the post alignment headed straight towards Flag Fen. Now we knew that there were posts west of our artificial lake, beside the car-park, under the Visitor Centre, and at two points on the lake's circumference. The posts then ran across the platform, through the main excavations, and presumably across the field on the east side of the Mustdyke, perhaps for 200 m (660 ft) up to the gravel of Northey. In all, there was probably 900 m (2970 ft), perhaps even a full kilometre (3300 ft)

84 *Fengate Power Station, 1989. Aerial view (looking west) of the excavations. The post alignment runs along the centre of the excavation.*

85 *Plan of the post alignment, with Ditches 8 and 9 beneath (dashed line). (Martin Redding.)*

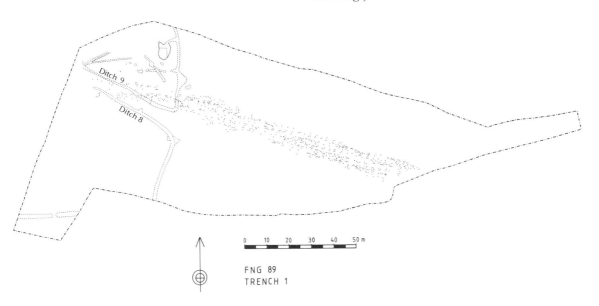

86 *The position of the highest posts was marked by garden canes. They can clearly be seen to form a broad alignment.*

of posts. It was an extraordinary thought.

The upright timbers in the main Flag Fen excavation were on the same alignment as the posts, but they were clearly of two types: large, slow-grown forest oak and much less substantial alder, or alternatively fast-grown oak. The former lined up along the walls and across the building and can be demonstrated by tree-ring analysis to be strictly contemporary with some of the *in situ* planks below them. These then are the timbers of the probable building, and possibly also of its replacement(s), too. We currently believe that the smaller oak posts and the structurally weak alders were part of the post alignment which actually, and doubtless deliberately, ran straight through the timbers of the original building. We strongly suspect that the building had by this point been abandoned, due to rising Fen water levels. It is a complex explanation, but the site itself is

extraordinarily complex: we currently estimate that there may be as many as four million pieces of wood in the post alignment and timber platform alone. As we will see, the explanation of Flag Fen is made no simpler by the recognition that it may not have been a simple domestic settlement, as we once believed; indeed, once ceremony and religion raise their heads, one can throw sweet reason out of the window.

The significance of tree-rings

The sorting out of the various episodes of building, rebuilding, post erection and replacement will depend to a very great extent on the technique of tree-ring analysis which will be playing a large role in the future of the Flag Fen project. This in turn depends on the simple fact that trees lay down wider growth-rings in good growing (usually wet) years than in poor ones. The width of each ring is measured through a microscope, to an accuracy of about a hundredth of a millimetre; the resulting graph of ring dimensions is then fed into a computer which already has information on tree-ring widths over the past 5000 years – and out pops a date. That, at least, is the principle – but there are snags.

Some trees, alder for example, may lay down two rings in a year, others grow slowly for most of the year and do not reflect the seasons. So the technique, known grandiloquently as *dendrochronology* ('dendro' for short), is mainly applied to oak, although ash can also be dated, and alder is reputed to be nearly sorted out in certain laboratories.

The 'dendro' at Flag Fen is done on-site by Janet Neve who joined us in 1984 after graduating in archaeology from Manchester University. Being a young and very poor project, we have not been able to offer Janet an instant and fully-fitted laboratory, but we have a rented portable office and plenty of enthusiasm. Janet has had the job of putting together the dendrometer, the machine that does the actual measuring (built for us by students at Peterborough Regional College from pieces of an RAF jet fighter, among other things), and the computer and its software (courtesy of Dr Pilcher at the Queen's University, Belfast). Assembling a 'dendro' laboratory on a shoe-

string is quite a challenge, but it is seldom boring, and now that Janet is beginning to produce results, it is all the more satisfying.

The technique of dendrochronology can give very accurate dates indeed and if bark is present it is possible to tell whether the tree was felled in the spring or autumn of any given year; yet it does not just provide accurate dates: dendro analysis also allows one to match timbers from the same tree and even to rebuild ancient patterns of forest management. At Flag Fen we hope it will help us sort out the problems of timber re-use and the complex patterns of rebuilding that are so evident in the main Flag Fen excavation. Already Janet has been able to demonstrate that at least some of the main

87 *A selection of small items, mostly bronze, mainly of Bronze Age and Early Iron Age date, found at Fengate Power Station. Note the fine brooch (top left), the spade-shaped razor (centre), three swan's neck pins (lower left) and numerous simple and spiral rings, some in pure tin.*

88 *Bronze shears and their wooden-box, probably Iron Age. Note the slot in the base of the box for the whetstone (not present when found). Shears similar to this are known in iron, but bronze shears of this antiquity are so far unique.*

oak posts are contemporary with the floor beneath – but that is just the start.

The summer of 1989 blazed on, and we had terrible problems trying to keep hundreds of posts wet. A routine, however, soon became established once we had secured the expert services of a small team of experienced excavators from the Lincoln Trust who dug and recorded the wood using the Flag Fen system. Poor Maisie and Janet ran from Flag Fen to the Power Station site in ever-decreasing circles, sampling, soaking and wrapping wood, but they survived – and were fitter for it.

The discovery of metalwork at the Power Station sub-site

Contrary to accepted archaeological opinion, I have always maintained that the vast majority of metal-detector users are honest people caught up in an absorbing hobby. Those who break the law are rogues and should be treated as such, but most are honestly doing amateur archaeology of a specialized sort. Rather than fight each other, archaeologists and metal-detector users should try to work together. Relations between the Soke Metal Detector Club and the Fenland Archaeological Trust have long been friendly. So in the spring of 1989 I invited the club to the Power Station site, as a normal routine visit. But I had a hunch that something remarkable was going to happen. Bronze Age metalwork and wet sites have long been known to go together, and before the search started, I told the group that they were looking for swords and daggers. This got a good laugh, but ten minutes later the laughter died when the first find, a sword, was revealed in the silts just to one side of the posts.

This discovery did wonders for my credibility.

I cannot attempt to recount the discovery of the metalwork piece by piece, as it all runs together in my mind as a bewildering, sun-baked, dusty rush around the site, desperately trying to keep on top of the mapping and note-taking. The club came back on the following five weekends and every time they found fresh material. By the first week in June we had nearly sixty objects, including two complete and two fragmentary swords (**colour plate 11**), numerous pins and other items (**87**), including an extraordinary pair of shears in a fitted wooden box (**88**). While the detecting was going on, the regular archaeological crew had also found two dog burials, one of which had been pierced by a post, and a human skeleton. Most of the metal finds were Late Bronze Age, but a significant number dated to the Early Iron Age – perhaps around 400–500 BC.

These finds were of great interest to David Keys of *The Independent* newspaper and he wrote a report which appeared on 24 June 1989. The story attracted widespread attention and did wonders to the Flag Fen visitor numbers, but it also caused, as I had anticipated, security problems on the Power Station excavation. So we never finished a day's work without an exhaustive metal-detector search and were at pains to remove everything of any value from the ground before we went home.

Finds of metalwork occurred at the very edge of the excavation and I realized that it was now time to expand the trench, and if needs be, on a huge scale. So we called on English Heritage who appeared on the scene bringing with them the large cheques we needed to pay potentially huge earthmoving bills. Our research design was elegant in its simplicity: keep removing earth until the archaeological finds stopped. No techniques can detect artefacts below more than 1 m ($3\frac{1}{4}$ ft) of topsoil, so we had no practical alternatives but to dig. The power station could not be delayed, so we had to move fast.

By the end of October we had cleared an area of about 2 ha (5 acres), with the posts running more-or-less down the centre. When we plotted where we had found the metalwork, it concentrated along the western side of the posts; very few finds were made on the other side (**89**). This completely ruled out the notion that the finds represented 'casual loss' from a road or raised causeway: even if we allow the absurd idea that Bronze Age people were the ultimate litter louts, one would expect 'casual losses' off a road to be evenly spread on either side.

Some of the items had been placed in the water about 30 m (99 ft) from the posts, and it

89 *Plan showing the distribution of Bronze and Iron Age metal artefacts around the post alignment (area shaded). (Martin Redding.)*

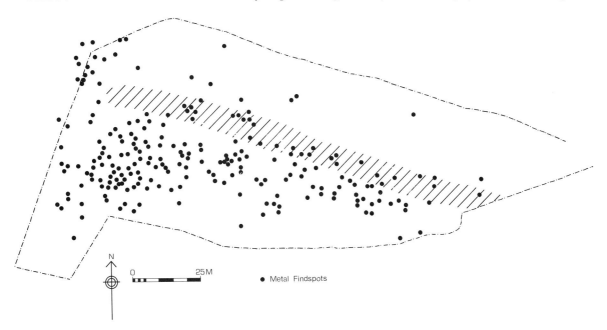

has been suggested that they might have been thrown there from a platform above the posts. I do not think this likely, however, because while many of the items had been broken, often broken pieces from the same item were found in the ground together – sometimes even touching. This could only happen if they had been either placed, or carefully dropped, in the water, probably from a boat.

The majority of items showed clear evidence of damage, indeed the conservator at the British Museum, Simon Dove, described it to me as prehistoric 'vandalism': pins were snapped in half; decorative inlay was smashed off; blades were bent and so on. One example will suffice. Dr David Coombs of Manchester University is an old friend and an acknowledged expert on Late Bronze Age metalwork. So when we started to excavate his subject matter by the

sackful I turned to him for help. Every few weekends he would call in to see what we had found. One Sunday morning he paid a flying visit and found us on site excavating around a metal-detector's very strong non-ferrous signal. Now David Coombs' doctoral thesis was on Late Bronze Age metalwork, and he has seen many thousands of bronzes, but this was the first time he had actually seen an axe come out of the ground; this is because Bronze Age metalwork is very rarely found in archaeological excavations: the vast majority are found by farmers, detectorists, quarrymen or old-fashioned navvies going about their daily business.

The bronze socketed axe that David and I excavated was in perfect condition and showed no signs of the 'vandalism' noted elsewhere – at least that is what we thought at first. But when we started to examine the wood round about the axe-head we soon saw that the two-piece handle had been smashed, leaving the axe itself intact. If one pauses to think about it, an axe is a difficult thing to smash – almost as hard as a hammer.

90 *A selection of tools, mainly Late Bronze Age, found at Fengate Power Station. Unhafted awls and piercers (left and top right); bone-hafted awl (centre right); and socketed gouge (lower right).*

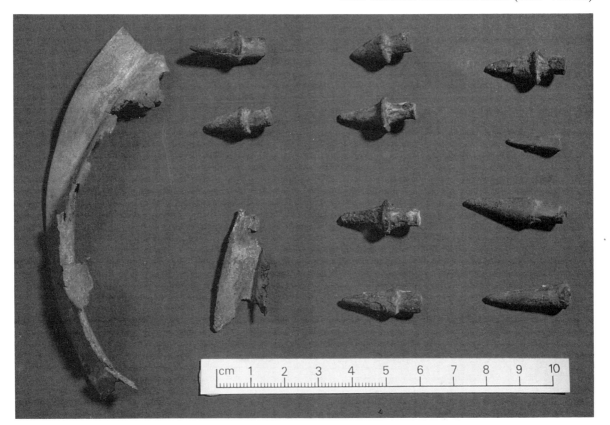

91 *Pieces of bronze from at least two Bronze Age helmets. To the left are two fragments of thin, beaten bronze, including part of the brim and crown; pointed rivets were used for decoration. (Derek Rootes.)*

So to sum up, the metalwork at the Power Station sub-site was found using detectors, a technique which is largely unbiased. The distribution of metalwork as revealed by the detectors is therefore a true reflection of its spread in antiquity in that it does not rely on something as fallible as eyesight. The vast majority of metal finds were amongst, and to one side of, the posts; again, most of the items were deliberately damaged and many had been carefully dropped, rather than thrown, into the water. These observations point indisputably to the fact that the metalwork, if nothing else, was deliberately removed from daily life by being deposited in the waters of Flag Fen. We will attempt to explain this seemingly irrational behaviour after a brief look at the collection.

The Power Station finds

The majority of metal items were in bronze, an alloy, usually of about 10 per cent tin and 90 per cent copper (brass, introduced to Britain in Roman times, also contains zinc). In all, there were just under 300 pieces of which the greatest number were pins, rings and ornaments; the greatest weight of metal, however, was in weapons: swords, dirks, daggers and a rapier. Tools were relatively rare, apart from a collection of almost twenty tanged chisels, punches and awls which were found in the same area and probably represent an individual craftsman's tool-kit (**90**).

Most of these objects dated to the Late Bronze Age and can be attributed to a well-defined style, group or 'industry' named after the Fenland village of Wilburton. Wilburton itself is on an old 'island', but the wet fen around it has produced large quantities of Late Bronze Age metalwork, in a very distinctive style – and all of it, I am quite convinced, put there on purpose. Two complete Wilburton swords were found at the Power Station, together with fragments of others and broken

92 *An artist's impression of a Bronze Age warrior in ceremonial dress. His clothes are based on finds from Danish bogs, his shoes are* *Dutch, but the metalwork is British. (Jo Richards.)*

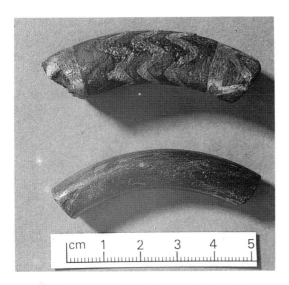

93 *Two fragments of shale armlet found near the post alignment. The top fragment has been finely inlaid with lead. (Derek Rootes.)*

pieces of scabbard fittings (**colour plate 11**). There was also a complete, but broken Early Iron Age sword (technically of La Tène I type) and pieces from others.

The collection of smaller-blade weapons was extraordinary, ranging from a complete Middle Bronze Age rapier, via sundry Late Bronze Age dirks and daggers to what can only be described as a miniature Wilburton sword (**colour plate 11**).

Late Bronze Age spears were less plentifully represented, but one spearhead, although partially sharpened was nonetheless incomplete, as the socket for its shaft was still filled with mould material; others still had pieces of wooden shaft in their sockets. The other end of many Bronze Age spears was tipped with a ferrule; generally these are quite small, but one very unusual large, broken example was also found.

It has been suggested that many Late Bronze Age shields and weapons found in bogs, fens and rivers were not functional. Professor John Coles has convincingly shown that the shafts of large spearheads were often too small to be used, and the thin bronze of shields would simply buckle and rip if struck hard by a Bronze Age sword. The same must apply to helmets, too. At least one, and possibly two were found and these are the first from Britain. Again, they

were smashed, but fragments of brim and crown metal survive, together with the long, pointed rivets that are so characteristic (**91**); the reconstruction is based on examples from France (**92**).

The most unusual find, and there are as yet no parallels for it in bronze, was a pair of sprung bronze shears in a carefully carved, fitted wooden box which had a little slot in the base for a sharpening stone (see **88**). These shears are probably of Iron Age date and can be used for shearing many things, from sheep to willow osiers.

There was a huge array of broken Bronze Age pins, mostly of stick type and with disc heads, some of which were decorated. Various rings in bronze and tin could have been ornaments or harness fittings and are entirely characteristic of the Late Bronze Age Wilburton tradition. Early Iron Age brooches, pins and ornaments were also bent, twisted or otherwise deliberately damaged, but were of very high class, often with provision for inlay of tin, glass or coral – most of which has sadly been smashed out (see **87**). It is perhaps worth noting that some of the Iron Age fine brooches are the type of item one would normally expect to find in a princely or warrior grave.

Arguably the most remarkable ornament was again smashed. Being unique it is hard to date at this stage, other than to state that it is probably Bronze Age. It is a large bracelet or armlet (a bracelet worn on the upper arm) of shale, but deeply inlaid with lead, which has been applied in strips (**93**). The decoration of bands, lozenges and chevrons is distinctly Bronze Age and can best be paralleled by a remarkable inlaid shale bowl of probable Late Bronze Age date, from Caergwrle, in the National Museum of Wales. It is a most exceptional object.

One extraordinary aspect of the Power Station sub-site discoveries is the fact that a proportion of the metal finds are of pure metallic tin. This has not been noted before in Britain, but is probably due to the site's naturally waterlogged conditions (which impede corosion) and the fact that most tin items are very small and unlikely to be spotted with the naked eye. An equally unusual find of a crucible fragment that had been used to melt pure tin, was made on the Cat's Water sub-site nearby, in 1975. This surely indicates that some of the Power Station finds were made locally, perhaps for the sole purpose of sacrifice to the waters.

This last suggestion might seem ridiculous were it not for the fact that many of the metal objects were clearly very second-rate castings. We have already referred to the spearhead with mould material still in its socket, but at least two of the swords had been broken across major casting flaws and one must ask whether they could ever have been used in actual battle. Similarly the miniature Wilburton sword is hardly an efficient fighting weapon. Could it be that much of this material was actually manufactured on site with deposition and ceremonial breakage in mind? This may not be as crazy as it sounds.

It would be a mistake to give the impression that metalwork was the only material found at the Power Station sub-site. There were many animal bones, often of dogs, and numerous potsherds, too. Whether these were deposited in the water along with the metalwork remains to be seen, however. Death is a recurrent theme: we have already mentioned a body, found on the north-eastern side of the posts, and two thigh bones of a fairly tall person were also found on that side, but some way away from the articulated bones. At one point an area of posts had been used to dispose of loose human bones; over three individuals are represented and with the bones we found a broken shale bracelet and a complete boar's tusk; these must surely be offerings of some sort.

Religion and ceremonial

It must be apparent that the Power Station site was a religious centre of some sort, but before we examine the possible nature of this religion we must consider the problem of what the site actually comprised. If, as we have already suggested, some of the posts at Flag Fen are part of the alignment is there evidence there also for religious activities? The answer is an assured yes.

This answer is based partly on a consideration of the metalwork: at the Power Station site it is principally composed of weapons and ornaments. At Flag Fen we have so far found one Iron Age brooch, a Late Bronze Age stick pin and a Late or Middle Bronze Age dagger. As at Fengate, these finds were amongst the posts or on their south-western side. The other distinctive items common to the two areas are smashed shale bracelets. At Flag Fen, too, we have evidence for careful deposition of pottery.

It has been suggested that there are far fewer metalwork finds at Flag Fen than at the Power Station, but in point of fact the former has produced slightly more on average, per square metre, than the latter. The balance of probability now indicates that the whole of the post alignment, including the section across Flag Fen, which could be 1 km ($\frac{3}{4}$ mile) in total length, is likely to be a huge religious monument.

Excavation during the long, hot summer of 1990 produced solid evidence that Flag Fen and the Fengate Power Station are all part of the same site. First, work with tree-rings demonstrated that a high proportion of the timbers from each area were growing at the same time. Second, as we penetrated to the lowest timbers at the main Flag Fen excavation we came across a bronze stick-pin of unusual continental type; a large socketed spearhead; and, most excitingly, the lower part of a scabbard, or chape. Like the Power Station finds of 1989, these were Late Bronze Age weapons or ornaments. There was nothing useful. Each item had been deliberately broken, and the spearhead had been carefully hidden beneath a large, axed log.

Rob Donaldson has painted a wonderfully imaginative view of a Flag Fen religious ceremony (**colour plate 12**). This scene, as I interpret it, depicts one of the grander rites and we are viewing the proceedings from amongst a large crowd. Perhaps scenes of this sort would only have taken place once or twice a year, whereas humbler individual or family ceremonies might well have taken place much more frequently. There can be little doubt that some of the broken items were dropped into the waters from a boat and by pure coincidence a Late Bronze Age dugout canoe (or logboat to give it its archaeological name) was found in the muds on the edge of the River Nene when another power station was being built in the 1950s. The power station has recently been demolished and the boat, which was once in Peterborough Museum, has since been burnt. As the photo taken at the time makes quite

94 *The Peterborough logboat, probably Late Bronze Age. Found during the construction of a power station in the 1950s. The bow section shown here measured 5 m (15 ft 9 in.). (Courtesy of Peterborough Museum.)*

clear, the Peterborough oak boat was a well made and sophisticated craft (**94**), quite appropriate for the kinds of ceremonial I am suggesting took place at Flag Fen.

Archaeologists have long been aware of the 'ritual' deposition of Bronze Age metalwork in wetlands. Incidentally, the term 'ritual' merely means that there is no obvious domestic, functional reason for the activity, which can otherwise only be explained in terms of religion or ceremonial. Now we cannot be certain that all of the many thousands of Bronze Age metalwork finds from the Fens got there during religious or sacrificial 'rituals', some might simply represent casual loss, others might have been hidden there for safety, but the sheer quantity of complete or deliberately damaged items found in the Fens is too enormous to support the idea that Bronze Age people were either absurdly forgetful or too lazy to keep track of their valuables. There is also a problem in deciding what parts of the Fen were indeed truly wet in the Bronze Age – many areas, for example, may well have been small dry islands. It is very easy when studying a region such as Fenland from outside, to treat it as all the same, whereas in reality, as we have seen, the apparently flat, featureless modern countryside hides a wealth of complex and highly diverse ancient landscapes.

So, having itemized reasons to be cautious, we are left with a core of unusual, apparently inexplicable, finds that must owe their existence in the Fen to religious or other 'rituals'. The main group of such 'ritual' finds is surely the weapons, many of which show clear signs of deliberate destruction.

The huge quantities and high quality of later Bronze Age metalwork recovered from the Fens and certain rivers of southern Britain (particularly the Thames) has led archaeologists recently to draw comparisons with the rich barrow burials of the preceding Neolithic and Early Bronze Ages. Maybe, it is argued, we are seeing here symbolic, if not actual burial of important people in the waters of rivers and fens. It should also be pointed out that this is not a phenomenon restricted to Britain alone, as Bronze Age metalwork is known from wetland situations over large areas of northern and Atlantic Europe – although nowhere are the quantities as great as in southern Britain.

The 'funerary' argument has much to recommend it, and at Flag Fen (we will include the Power Station site with Flag Fen for present purposes) we can demonstrate that death featured prominently. I am sure that the smashed black shale bracelets and armlets might well have had some funerary significance. On the other hand I also think there was more to what went on at Flag Fen than merely the disposal or remembrance of the dead. For a start, thanks to metal detectors we have, for the first time, an idea of the enormous variety of metalwork that was deposited in the waters. This surely must indicate both a range of people and a range of activities: there are magnificent items doubtless worth the modern equivalent of vast sums of money and there are humbler items, maybe worth much less.

The key to understanding what might have been going on lies in the broken state of so many objects. Prior to the Middle Bronze Age, grave goods in barrows may include weapons and ornaments, but they are rarely, if ever, deliberately smashed. This is something new. It may well have an underlying economic purpose. Professor Richard Bradley has suggested that metal was being withdrawn from circulation to keep prices high, but this was probably not in the forefront of peoples' minds at the time. Furthermore, the destruction of something valuable in the naturally open surroundings of water is essentially a public act, and one which could be interpreted as a display of wealth and prestige.

Conclusion

It would seem then that the 'ritual' ceremonies at Flag Fen were often about death, but they were also about life: the competition for social status amongst most, if not all, members of the community. The rites seemed to have started in the Middle Bronze Age, and may well be associated with the construction of the extraordinary timber platform in the middle of the slowly wettening fen. It was positioned midway between the dryland of Fengate and that of Northey to the east. To the north-east lay the open Fen and to the south-west the floodplain of the Nene and the flat, fertile land of Fengate. The platform stood at the boundary between four quite distinct worlds; it must always have been a place of importance. Perhaps the buildings on the platform were not simply dwellings, as we originally thought, but were instead halls or public buildings, visited on special occasions. Then, as conditions grew wetter, it became impossible to use the platform and its public building(s), but its boundary function was expressed formally by the posts, which eventually ran right across it.

These were the grand things that were going on at Flag Fen: the eternal verities of life, such as power, politics and prestige. But there was another side that I touched on at the close of the last chapter. Flag Fen has produced swords and daggers, rapiers and helmets, even beautiful encrusted bronze and shale jewellery. But what about those countless little things, the stick-pins, the razors, the knives and other scrappy items too insignificant to describe in any detail? What about the meat bones and the pottery? Why were these things deliberately broken and dropped into the waters, along with the more spectacular, prestigious stuff?

I would suggest that the reasons for the disposal of these simpler things lie with them in the water. In some cases we may guess at them from their appearance: perhaps a razor was offered to the waters at the onset of manhood, a fine pin for a lover, hand tools after completing a hard apprenticeship and so on. We must not forget that these people were individuals like us: doubtless they would also have thrown coins in the fountain, if they had had them. Perhaps the waters of Flag Fen brought special good fortune in love, in the hunt or in any other important aspect of life. Some of the items must have been dropped into the waters with cheering crowds and much rejoicing; others might have marked the end of a long and distinguished life; still others were doubtless private acts of longing, regret or recrimination. All of human life is there, had

we the power to see it.

It is interesting that the metal finds are concentrated on the western or Nene valley side of the posts; this might indicate that the people came from that direction – as opposed to the Fen-edge further north. The evidence is slight, but two bodies or parts of bodies were found on the sea- or fen-ward side of the posts; the symbolic significance of this is quite plain.

It has been suggested that people pay special attention to their boundaries in times of tension and we have argued that the posts represent a boundary. If the population had indeed been increasing throughout the Bronze Age, and water levels were inexorably rising across Fenland, this would inevitably exacerbate any existing tribal tensions. On the other hand, tension of that sort might be indicated by religious ceremonial on both sides of the boundary. Perhaps in this case the enemy beyond the posts is the sea itself, for by the succeeding Iron Age huge areas of fen were inundated by salt water. It must have been a very frightening process indeed for local communities. Even today Fen people fear sea floods more than any other natural or political disaster.

The focus of religious activity seems to have moved higher up the Nene by the end of the Iron Age, when a series of magnificent swords and scabbards were thrown into the river at Orton Longueville, on the west side of Peterborough. By this stage Flag Fen was a huge expanse of water and the posts had long since vanished; but the fundamental belief, that of throwing valuable weapons into water, persisted – a thousand years after Flag Fen.

6

The Iron Age (700 BC-AD 43)

From Bronze to Iron

Our story is drawing to a close, and for the first time we begin to see glimpses of a more familiar world. In many respects the countryside of Iron Age Britain was similar to that of post-Roman England, with small villages and scattered farmsteads. True, the network of formal Roman roads was not yet in existence, but the roadways that did exist were perfectly adequate for the task, if perhaps a little less straight, but that only matters to people in a hurry. But we must be very careful not to assume that a landscape which was superficially similar to landscapes of modern Britain or Ireland was peopled by folk more or less similar to us. True, they would have looked like us, but their society would still have been very different from ours. A proper study of the Iron Age should not look for ways in which 'they resembled us'; that is a very arrogant way to carry on. Should we not rather wonder (and regret) why we resemble them so little?

For purposes of argument, we shall treat the Iron Age as beginning at around 500 BC, since the two centuries or so before that are not too clearly understood and the evidence is rather thin on the ground in our area, apart, that is, from the very earliest Iron Age finds at the Power Station sub-site. Two of these finds, however, were not mentioned in the previous chapter. The first is a bronze sword, broken in two pieces and dated to a period known on the continent as 'Hallstatt C'. In mainland Europe this is the first true Iron Age period, but in England it is usually treated as the ultimate Bronze Age, or transitional between the Bronze and Iron Ages. In addition to a bronze sword of Iron Age type we also have an iron axe of Bronze Age type; sadly this iron socketed axe

is very corroded, but these two items illustrate that there was no real break between the Ages. So let us treat the years 700 to 500 BC as essentially Late Bronze Age, and resume our story in the Iron Age proper.

The Iron Age landscape of lowland eastern England is characterized by small farmsteads and hamlets set in ditched and hedged fields and pastures, which are often linked together by droveways and tracks. There would have been far more woodland then than now, but otherwise the landscape bore at least a passing resemblance to that of today.

Any view of prehistory inevitably tends to stress how things are progressing: from caves and skins, via chariots to cars and ultimately spaceships. The people of every archaeological period, however, lived their lives very much influenced by their own history, just as we do today. Their ideas of time were undoubtedly more cyclical or seasonal than today, but by the Iron Age people in southern Britain had been living within an organized countryside for at least three and a half thousand years. In that time they must have developed a view of their own past which (like our own view of history was part myth, part reality) must have played a major role in shaping their actions. Accordingly we must beware of assuming that they must always have acted like us, only more ancient. Two thousand five hundred years is a very long time indeed and I suspect we would find life in the Iron Age far stranger than just living in a round-house and eating off coarse

95 *Flag Fen 1990: lowering the synthetic roof on the reconstructed Cat's Water sub-site Iron Age house.*

pottery. We might well find that their whole system of beliefs, standards and values was based on a view of history that was entirely alien to us. So this is probably an appropriate place to say a few words about our own attempts to recreate the past experimentally.

In chapter 4 I described how we recreated a Bronze Age round-house within its original fields, but this was only an 'experiment' insofar as the roof was concerned; the rest was fairly straightforward and based on pioneering work by Peter Reynolds at the Little Butser experimental Iron Age farm, near Petersfield in Hampshire. Having said that, I personally have quite serious qualms about some of the con-

structional techniques we employed: I find it hard to believe, knowing what I do about the sophistication of prehistoric carpentry, for example, that so much use was made of crude lashing. Prehistoric sites rarely produce evidence for twine or cordage, and yet our buildings used it extensively. We do our best, but the most we can hope to achieve is just a very crude approximation of what might have existed in the past. I am not aware that we have ever over-estimated the abilities or sophistication of prehistoric people – we reserve that for ourselves.

The Bronze Age building presented more technical problems than the Iron Age building erected in 1990. This house was based on one found in the Cat's Water settlement (to be described below). The building enclosed an area 10 m (33 ft) in diameter and the apex of the roof was 6 m (18 ft) above the ground. We decided

96 *A selection of Late Iron Age safety-pin type bronze brooches and a complete wheel-made jar.*

97 *A general view of the Cat's Water Iron Age settlement during excavation. Note the circular eaves-drip ditches of round-houses.*

not to finish it properly, using thatch, sedge and daub, but instead roofed it with a synthetic material that allows one to appreciate the complexities of even our imperfect carpentry (**95** and **96**).

Some experimentalists have attempted to work out man-hours spent erecting prehistoric houses, Stonehenges, or whatever. These worthy attempts are inevitably doomed to failure for many reasons; only two really matter. Firstly, they ignore the many thousands of years experience available to the ancient craftsmen; secondly they assume that people actually wanted to build things efficiently, in a cost-effective way. Maybe there was a method people used, even though they knew that it could be done more efficiently some other way. The best one can do is replicate a process and say that this is how long it might have taken, plus or minus an unknown time – and that is not much use at all.

The archaeological record of the Iron Age is marked by a sharp increase in the quantity of pottery found on excavations. By this period people were beginning to understand far better how to control and use fire. Iron smelting (the actual extraction of the metal from the ore) required sustained high temperatures and a degree of control that is hard to replicate experimentally today, unless one has a fair knowledge of metallurgy. This greater understanding of pyrotechnology was not confined to the metalworkers and smiths alone, for pottery improves by leaps and bounds by the end of the Middle Iron Age, around 200 BC. Not only are the ceramics better fired and harder, but they were produced in much greater quantities. The next technological breakthrough took place in the Late Iron Age, towards the end of the first century BC, with the introduction of the potter's wheel.

The Iron Age at Fengate

Iron Age activity at Fengate between 500 and 300 BC is confined to two main areas. The first is much closer to Peterborough and was revealed by Wyman Abbott before the Second World War. It consisted of a number of deep pits which contained large quantities of pottery, now in Peterborough Museum. These pits were once thought to have been individually filled in one operation, but as we saw in chapter 2, this was probably not the case. Other than that rather negative comment, it is difficult to say anything intelligent about this site.

The second site was located further inland, on the Vicarage Farm sub-site. The subsoil was Cornbrash, a type of crumbly limestone, which had been quite severely eroded by ploughing, so that very shallow archaeological evidence had been destroyed. This probably explains the absence of house foundations and other slight features, such as stake- and post-holes. The commonest features were pits, some of them deep enough to be 'sock' wells and many had pottery thrown into them; in this respect the Vicarage Farm settlement resembled that discovered by Abbott. Some of the pottery was rather remarkable, including a unique sherd with chalky inlaid decoration, and another with a finely-made, wrapped wooden handle.

The pits and hollows of the Vicarage Farm settlement were grouped together, which suggests that they once belonged to a farmstead or small hamlet and there was some evidence for 'settlement drift', whereby the community gradually moved across the land, perhaps covering 100 m (330 ft) in two centuries. Assuming that it really was 'settlement drift', and not the chance relocation of several intermittent, short-lived settlements, then it was hardly rapid.

The principal Iron Age settlement was located on the Cat's Water sub-site, much nearer the Fen and just 300 m (990 ft) southwest of the Power Station post-alignment's landfall. Its discovery, although slightly less dramatic than Flag Fen, is also of some interest; again, 'luck' was on our side.

The well-known aerial photograph of Fengate, published in the 'Peterborough Volume', shows two droveway ditches (see 12) running diagonally across the picture, from east to west. The droveway ended in a distinct series of ditched farmyards, and a scatter of locally-made Roman pottery on the field surface in that area, strongly suggested the presence of a Romano-British farm below the surface. So when we started to excavate the ditched farmyards, in 1975, we thought things were going to be straightforward enough.

It was at about this time that Dr Paul Craddock of the British Museum Research Laboratory first contacted us for a suitable site to test his soil phosphate analyses. We have seen how successful they were on Bronze Age droveways, but we also wanted to see how well they worked in an actual farmyard, where concentrations were likely to be very much higher. The Cat's Water site seemed ideal, as it looked so simple: we would be able to get a clear, single-period picture without 'background noise' and other interference caused by later or earlier activity in the same area. At least, that is what we fondly hoped.

Dr Craddock arrived with a team of trainees from a local Detention Centre. The work was hard, as each sample involved hand-drilling through stiff clay, and the conditions were pretty unpleasant, but Paul and his team did a splendid job. When the results were plotted out, to our amazement the area of highest phosphate was outside the ditched farmyards. This seemed to make no sense whatsoever, but the results were very definite and could not be shrugged off.

I then retrieved as many air photos as I could find and took a much closer look at the land immediately north of the ditched yards. With the eye of faith I could just make out one or two faint, ghost-like ditches, which we now know were lying, partially obscured, beneath Roman flood clay. I am quite convinced that we would have missed them entirely had Paul Craddock and his team not done their work. So we started our excavation well to the north of the main yards, on the off-chance that the phosphate tests and faint cropmarks would tell an interesting story.

The overburden was thick and difficult to machine, especially when wet, so we had to resort to heavy-duty equipment – motorway scrapers with bulldozer assistance – and I was very concerned lest we might cause damage. However, we were able to use more gentle machines once the stiff flood clay had been removed, and there, just a little below the clay, were the remains of a buried Iron Age hamlet. It was this, and not the few ditches that showed up through the flood clay, which had raised the soil phosphate levels – and little wonder, for there was archaeology everywhere. I had never seen so many pits, post-holes, gullies and ditches, all of which showed up as dark marks in the exposed subsoil.

Following the success of the phosphate survey, we arranged with the Detention Centre for a party of six to eight trainees to come and dig. In addition to the actual trainees, there were supervisory staff such as van drivers, all of whom joined in; in effect, it meant that we had at our disposal an extra ten to twelve excavators – approximately double our regular workforce. This influx of new people saved the day, because we now had one team of a dozen working on the Bronze Age ditched fields, and another of the same size (or very slightly larger) working at Cat's Water, where the quantities of finds and features threatened to engulf us all. Our deadlines were real, as factories now stand where once we had been digging, and the

pressure was all-pervasive. Everyone was in a state of collapse at the end of each day.

The Fengate Cat's Water Iron Age settlement was dug between 1975 and 1978. It consisted of about 55 buildings in all, of which about ten would have been in use at the same time (**97**). Of these ten buildings, five were for people, and five for livestock. The floor area of the houses would not have been large enough to have accommodated more than a single, or nuclear family consisting of parents and their children, so we must imagine a small hamlet of five houses and perhaps 30 people in all. The houses were grouped quite tightly together, and the whole settlement: houses, barns, animal byres, ditches and yards did not occupy much more than 1 ha (2.5 acres) of land.

98 *Model of part of the Cat's Water Iron Age settlement. (Eric Ricketts and David Rayner. Courtesy of Peterborough Museum.)*

99 *The Fen Causeway Roman road shows as a parch-mark in growing cereal crops. (S.J. Upex, Nene Valley Research Committee.)*

The houses were round, walled in woven wattle and plastered with 'daub' – clay mixed with chopped straw or cow dung. Sometimes we found direct evidence for the walling; in one or two cases buildings, or parts of buildings, had caught fire and the daub had become fired, rather like pottery. Its self-firing was fuelled by the wattle and the chopped straw mixed in it; after it had been fired it retained its shape, with the wattlework impressions clearly visible.

Unlike the round-houses of the Bronze Age, the Iron Age structures on Cat's Water were probably thatched with local reed (see **98**). We have found the foundations of several dozen such buildings, but never any evidence for the stout internal posts required to support a turf roof. It has been suggested that the internal roof-support posts were not sunk into the ground, since they are only required to carry a vertical load. It is also argued that the ground water-table (which we know was high in the Late Iron Age) would soon rot the posts; so it would be sensible not to sink them unless it was absolutely necessary. However, having now constructed two round houses, one with, and one without roof-support posts, I am convinced that internal posts must be earthfast and not free-standing, particularly when several people are scrambling around on the roof, laying turf or thatch. I also find it highly improbable that all evidence for them had vanished; in reality, I think we have evidence for an important change in constructional technique.

Burnt mud walls and pottery were not the only items in fired clay to be found: we also found many triangular weights, weighing, when complete, about 1 kg (2¼ lb) each. There is some doubt about the function of these weights, which are usually perforated at the corners; some archaeologists would interpret them as thatch weights, or net sinkers, but these explanations are impractical: logs or rocks make the best thatch weights (which have to be very heavy, as anyone who has ever sheeted a haystack in a gale will tell you), and stones make the best net sinkers, as water will soon penetrate and weaken such poorly fired

clay. The most reasonable explanation is that these weights were used in looms, to provide tension for the vertical threads (warps).

Every Iron Age settlement site produces a mass of fired clay, and frequently it is impossible to decide on its original use – if any. But at Fengate we were fortunate to have better than usual preservation and most objects were found in the ground more or less where they had been dropped, or placed, in antiquity. One large mass of fired clay lumps and chunks was reassembled into a flued oven, with a central fire-hole, a lower storey fire-box and an upper storey oven which was given additional heat by a number of smaller fire-holes or perforations through the oven floor.

The ditched fields and droveways of the Bronze Age had been abandoned for about 700 years when the Cat's Water settlement was first built, somewhere around 300 BC. The earlier banks and ditches must have been barely, if at all, visible and the only trace of the previous landscape might have been an occasional huge oak tree that survived in an out-of-the-way hedge. Charles French analysed the snails in the bottom of Iron Age ditches at Cat's Water and showed them to be very much wetter than their Bronze Age antecedents; we must imagine them lined with reeds and probably choked with sedge and pondweed.

The Bronze Age way of life was based on livestock with droveways running down to the Fen; people lived in single family settlements dotted around their fields. The later Iron Age hamlet at Cat's Water could not be more different: if anything, its yards faced away from the Fen and its ditches disregarded the arrangement of the earlier landscape. In many respects the change of landscape 'style' was greater than that between the earliest Neolithic and the Bronze Age proper, discussed in chapters 3 and 4. This change of landscape mirrored a change in the local economy away from livestock, to a more balanced pattern of mixed farming.

Iron Age villagers at Cat's Water grew wheat and barley on the higher, flood-free land back from the Fen – most probably around the land now occupied by Perkins Engines' enormous diesel engine factory, north and west of the Vicarage Farm sub-site. There is not much direct evidence for cereals – a few grains and fragments of chaff – but this is not altogether surprising, given the settlement's very low-lying position. Wheat and barley do not tolerate being flooded during their growing season, and as the Iron Age Fenland was very wet, this might well account for the rarity of direct evidence. We did, however, discover numerous sherds of large vessels that are generally thought to be grain storage jars, and the eaves-drip gully of one round-house produced a near-complete quernstone (millstone), made from Lincolnshire limestone.

Apart from cereals, the inhabitants of Iron Age Fengate grew apples (pips were found) and vegetables probably included celery, mustard leaves and parsnips; thyme might have been used as a strewing or culinary herb. I use the word 'probably' because it is very hard indeed to distinguish early cultivars from wild species – and it is quite possible that unimproved wild species were actually grown. The main weed of modern sugarbeet fields, for example, is fat hen or *Chenopodium album*. This plant was found in archaeological features at Cat's Water and makes quite a palatable green vegetable when cooked like spinach.

The meadows of the Fen-edge around the settlement would have provided grazing for cattle, sheep, goats and pigs. Some wild animals were still hunted – a few deer, for example – and fishing also took place (large pike jaw-bones were found during the excavations). I suspect, however, that the available archaeological evidence tends to underestimate the importance of fish in the Iron Age and earlier prehistoric diet. The problem of finding archaeological evidence for fishing illustrates the problems of interpreting bone evidence in general: we have to assume that the material we find on site is broadly speaking representative of what actually took place there in the past. Sometimes this may not be a correct assumption to make.

Rotting fish remains stink, attract flies and are generally unpleasant. On the other hand, they are quite easy to dispose of in water, under a scoop of sand, in pig feed, or whatever. The bones themselves are generally small and do not survive particularly well, especially on sites with acid soils. Iron Age drainage ditches of the Cat's Water settlement produced 34 bones or fragments of pike, 9 of tench and 31 of bream. Incidentally, these fish could not have died in the ditches, unaffected by man, for the simple reason that they were never represented by complete skeletons, but just by single loose bones. This suggests that they were discarded with other household rubbish. A total of around 80 bones is hardly a significant collection, but I cannot believe that a settlement located on the very edge of the Fen, at one of the wettest periods in its history, could have ignored such a vitally important source of winter protein. It must therefore be under-representative; in reality I would not be surprised if during the winter the Iron Age villagers of Cat's Water caught fish and eels by the hundredweight. The problem is proving it.

Prehistoric Fengate must have been an ornithologist's dream. The Iron Age and Roman deposits at Cat's Water produced bones of the following: goose, mallard, pelican, cormorant, heron, stork, mute swan, barnacle goose, teal, tableduck, merganser, sea eagle, goshawk, hawk, buzzard, crane, coot and crow (two species). Most were probably eaten, since they are represented, like the fish, by loose bones in amongst domestic refuse.

It would appear that in the later Iron Age people ate a diet that was not radically unlike that of pre-drainage days, around 400 years ago. But there were other products of the Fen that folk also could use: willow bark, for example, could be boiled up to make a rather soporific, pain-relieving aspirin 'tea'. However there is also evidence for stronger medicines: seeds of opium poppy were found in late Iron Age or early Roman soils in one of the settlement's ditches. Opium-derived medicines were traditionally used in the Fens to relieve the pains of malaria which was endemic until very recently.

So to sum up, although the Cat's Water settlement was positioned at the edge of the true wetland, it would still have been very damp by modern standards, and this we have tried to show in the excellent model made shortly after the site's excavation (**98**). The model shows a small part of the settlement, with the building on the left serving as a cattle shed; that to the right is a house.

The people who lived at Cat's Water, like many other Iron Age communities in Britain did not dispose of their dead in a very archaeologically-visible fashion: for example, there was no formally-defined cemetery area. The body of a child was buried in the crouched position in a house eaves-drip gully, whereas the other five intact burials were all crammed into small pit-like graves, tightly crouched up; one was even squeezed into a sack or bag. All were either teenagers or young adults in their twenties. Three cremations, in small pits, were also recovered. This rather sad catalogue is greatly increased by finds of loose human bones mixed in with animal bones, pottery and general debris from pits, ditches and other settlement features of the hamlet. It is hard to interpret these loose bones: some could derive from graves that had been disturbed, but they are so commonly encountered on settlement sites of the Iron Age in Britain that some kind of 'exposure' or excarnation burial has been suggested. Perhaps a body was placed on a platform, rather than in the ground, and when the flesh had rotted was considered to have no further special significance. Whatever actually happened, a lot of bodies were disposed of: even if only 30 people occupied the site at any one time we must suppose a total population of several hundred individuals over 300 or so years. They would provide a fair quantity of loose bones, but we found just 20, including bits, pieces and fragments. I suspect the majority of the adult dead were buried away from the settlement, either alone, or in unmarked cemeteries – out in Flag Fen perhaps?

The coming of the Romans
The final episode of our story can be briefly stated. The Roman military authorities took a road from the then small market town at *Durobrivae*, ran it across the land where Peterborough now stands, over to the Fen-edge in Fengate (**99** and see **13**). They then 'island hopped' the road from Fengate to Northey and Whittlesey, Coates and March, ultimately leaving the wetlands at the Norfolk fen-edge

town of Denver, at which point the Fen Causeway joins the larger Norfolk system. The road is widely thought to have been built as part of the crushing of Boudica's revolt of AD 60/61, and whether this is true or not, it was certainly built sometime in the later first century AD. One might expect it to have had some effect on the Cat's Water settlement, which it brushed by; but apparently it did not.

The Cat's Water settlement continued into Roman times up until the third century AD, when widespread freshwater flooding throughout the southern Fenlands caused people to seek higher and safer ground. Happily for the buried archaeological remains, people have stayed clear of the area until recent times when we, in our infinite wisdom, have seen fit to drain and develop.

Postscript
When we bought our first micro-computer, in 1979, we were told by everyone 'wait until 1980, silicon chips will be cheaper and faster'. When we replaced that machine with a more modern one, five years ago, we were told to wait, as the IBM system was sure to be replaced by something even better. In both cases we made the right decision, but now I am told, 'don't write your book until you have all the tree-ring dates available', and 'put nothing in print until you have dug more of the platform'. Even then someone will think of something else to delay us. The point is this: no archaeological book is ever the final word, just as no archaeological interpretation is ever correct. In the final analysis, archaeology is a humanity and archaeologists, alas, are only too human.

Appendix

Places to visit in Peterborough and the surrounding area

The Fengate sites now lie beneath factory buildings and most of the important archaeological sites of the Fens lie on private land. Apart from Flag Fen itself, there is almost nothing of prehistoric age visible for the interested visitor. The area is, however, extraordinarily rich in architecture and several days can profitably be spent looking at the many fine buildings and townscapes.

Flag Fen excavations

Flag Fen itself is open to the public every day of the year, except Christmas Day and Boxing Day. The park and Visitor Centre open at 11.00 a.m. and close at 5.30 p.m. or dusk (in winter). There is a gift shop and cafeteria in the Visitor Centre. During the excavation season (Easter to the end of October), the first guided tour is at 11.30 a.m., the last at 4.00 p.m. There are no guided tours outside the excavation season, but the park, Visitor Centre and displays are open. Further information (including admission prices) can be obtained on application to Flag Fen Excavations, Fourth Drove, Peterborough PE1 5UR (tel. 0733-313414). The site is located in Peterborough's Eastern Industrial Area Ordnance Survey Map 142, Grid Reference TL 227989. There are at least six other Flag Fens in Fenland, including one at Whittlesey which appears prominently on Ordnance Survey Maps. So do not be misled! The site is clearly signed from the Peterborough ring-road (A1139).

There is much to see at Flag Fen and we normally recommend that visitors allow themselves at least an hour-and-a-half for a visit.

Peterborough is only 50 minutes from London's King's Cross station and there is a regular service from York and the North. There are also direct rail links with Leicester and the Midlands, Cambridge, Norwich and East Anglia. The bus service to Flag Fen is infrequent (Viscount Bus 30, Queensgate Bus Centre) and involves a half-mile walk. We suggest visitors coming by rail take a taxi to the site.

Peterborough Museum and Art Gallery

(Priestgate, Peterborough. Tel. 0733-443329. Closed Sundays and Mondays.)

Peterborough Museum is notable for its collection of bone carvings made by Napoleonic prisoners of war. It also has a fine collection of prehistoric material from Fengate.

Peterborough Cathedral

Undoubtedly the least-known of Britain's great ancient cathedrals. It is mainly Norman, but with a very unusual Early English west front. It is also unspoiled by over-restoration or a profusion of memorials, and has one of the finest painted nave ceilings in Europe. Monastic buildings surround the cathedral and the Close is particularly fine.

Longthorpe Tower

(English Heritage, open all year round; OS map 142, Grid Reference TL 163983) Situated on the old A47 3 km (2 miles) west of the city, Longthorpe Tower is an outstanding example of a fortified fourteenth century manor house tower. Its medieval wall paintings are remarkable.

The Peterborough District

Outside Peterborough the visitor can go in three directions, all within a half-hour's drive of the city centre. To the north, along the A1, lie Burghley House, built by Queen Elizabeth I's Chancellor, the Marquis of Exeter, and Stamford, arguably the finest stone-built small town in England.

To the west of Peterborough the rolling limestone countryside includes a number of beautiful stone-built villages, including Wansford, with its medieval road bridge and fine coaching inns; Barnack and Castor, both with magnificent churches (one Saxon, the other Norman) and Fotheringay, best known as the place where Mary, Queen of Scots was beheaded (the castle where this took place has largely disappeared). The small stone-built town of Oundle is also worth visiting. Elton Hall is famous for its sumptuous decor, distinguished pictures and refurbished gardens.

To the east of Peterborough lie the Fens whose wide open vistas are well worth viewing for themselves. The Fens were famed for their monastic sites (both Peterborough and Ely cathedrals were once monastic churches) and the smaller churches at Crowland, Thorney and Ramsey are all worth visiting. Crowland also boasts an unusual triangular bridge – the Trinity Bridge. Slightly further east, the church of St Wendreda, March, has the finest carved angel roof in Britain, and the town of Wisbech, near the mouth of the River Nene, has a superb Georgian river frontage; the gardens of Peckover House (National Trust) are lovely.

Further reading

General

Although written before the discovery of Flag Fen, and now rather outdated, the following is still a useful introduction to Fengate: Pryor, F.M.M. (1982), *Fengate*, Shire Archaeology (Princes Risborough).

The Fengate campaigns of 1971–78 are comprehensively covered in four reports; the first is mainly devoted to a Neolithic 'house', middle Iron Age pits at Padholme Road and an early Iron Age settlement at Vicarage Farm: Pryor, F.M.M. (1974), *Excavation at Fengate, Peterborough, England: the First Report*. Royal Ontario Museum Archaeology Monograph 3 (Toronto).

The second report is entirely given over to a Late Neolithic site on the Storey's Bar Way sub-site: Pryor, F.M.M. (1978), *Excavation at Fengate, Peterborough, England: The Second Report*. Royal Ontario Museum Archaeology Monograph 5 (Toronto).

The third report considers the Bronze Age drove and enclosure system, with special reference to the Newark Road sub-site: Pryor, F.M.M. (1980), *Excavation at Fengate, Peterborough, England: the Third Report*. Northamptonshire Archaeological Society Archaeological Monograph 1/Royal Ontario Museum Archaeology Monograph 6 (Toronto and Leicester).

The fourth report covers the large Middle and Late Iron Age settlement at Cat's Water, a Neolithic multiple burial, also at Cat's Water and remaining Iron Age features at Vicarage Farm: Pryor, F.M.M. (1984), *Excavation at Fengate, Peterborough, England: the Fourth Report*. Northamptonshire Archaeological Society Archaeological Monograph 2/Royal Ontario Museum Archaeological Monograph 7 (Toronto and Leicester).

Flag Fen is treated in one detailed report to date: Pryor, F.M.M.; French, C.A.I. and Taylor, M. (1986), 'Flag Fen, Fengate Peterborough I: Discovery, Reconnaissance and Initial Excavation (1982–85)' *Proceedings of the Prehistoric Society* 42, 1–24.

More recent research at Flag Fen and the Fengate Power Station sub-site is covered in the following: Scottish Archaeological Review 1990; Antiquity special section 1991; *Current Archaeology* No. 119 (1990), 386–90.

1 The Fens

Mellows, W.T. (ed.) (1966), *The Peterborough Chronicle of Hugh Candidus* 2nd (revised) edition, Peterborough Museum and Art Gallery.

The formation and geography of the Fens are treated in the following good general accounts, with copious references: Godwin, H. (1978), *Fenland: its Ancient Past and Uncertain Future*, Cambridge University Press. Darby, H.C. (1983), *The Changing Fenland*, Cambridge University Press.

The standard work on the Roman Fenland: Phillips, C.W. (1970), *The Fenland in Roman Times*, Royal Geographical Society, Research Series, No. 5, London.

Anglo-Saxon sea defences and Marshland in general, with many references: Silvester, R.J. (1988), *The Fenland Project, Number 3: Norfolk Survey, Marshland and Nar Valley*, East Anglian Archaeology, 45, Norwich.

Medieval and Saxon drainage and embankment, with many references: Hall, D.N. (1987), *The Fenland Project, Number 2: Cambridgeshire Survey, Peterborough to March*, East Anglian Archaeology, 35, Cambridge.

Fenland drainage. A huge subject, Darby is the standard work; Hills is excellent on mechanical engineering; both with many references: Darby, H.C. (1940), *The Draining of the Fens,* Cambridge University Press. Hills, R.L. (1967), *Machines, Mills and Uncountable Costly Necessities,* Goose, Norwich.

Modern sensitive wetland management: Purseglove, J. (1988), *Taming the Flood,* Oxford University Press/Channel 4 Books.

Preservation of an archaeological site in a nature reserve; also an excellent archaeological read: Coles, B.J. and J.M. (1986), *Sweet Track to Glastonbury,* Thames and Hudson, London.

2   Archaeology in the Peterborough area

Aerial photography. The first is general, the second a series of case-studies: Duel, L. (1969), *Flights into Yesterday,* Macdonald, London. Wilson, D.R. (1975), *Aerial Reconnaissance for archaeology,* Council for British Archaeology Research Report No. 12.

For earthworms and other archaeological soil matters: Limbrey, S. (1975), *Soil Science and Archaeology,* Academic Press, London and New York.

General Pitt-River's biography: Thompson, M.W. (1977), *General Pitt-Rivers,* Moonraker Press, Bradford-on-Avon.

Professor Grimes pioneered open area excavation; the report is a masterpiece: Grimes, W.F. (1960), *Excavations of Defence Sites, 1939–45. I: Mainly Neolithic-Bronze Age,* H.M.S.O., London.

Archaeological earthmoving, techniques and pitfalls: Pryor, F.M.M. (1986), *Earthmoving on Open Archaeological Sites,* Institute of Field Archaeologists Technical Paper, No. 4, Birmingham.

The philosophy behind the Flag Fen public display: Pryor, F.M.M. (1989), "Look What We've Found" – a case study in public archaeology' *Antiquity,* 63, 51–61.

The Peterborough area in Roman times: Wild, J.P. (1974), 'Roman Settlement in the Lower Nene Valley' *Archaeological Journal,* 131, 140–70.

Longthorpe, the Roman fortress: Frere, S.S. and St Joseph, J.K. (1974), 'The Roman Fortress at Longthorpe' *Britannia,* 5, 1–129.

Longthorpe, the military and civilian activity outside the fortress: Dannell, G.B. and Wild, J.P. (1987), *Longthorpe II,* Britannia Monograph Series, No. 8, London.

Date of the Cat's Water: Evans, R. (1979), 'The early courses of the river Nene' *Durobrivae,* 7, 8–10, Peterborough.

The five main references to Peterborough's prehistory, in chronological order: Abbott, G.W., and Smith, R.A. (1910), 'On the Discovery of Prehistoric Pits at Peterborough', *Archaeologia,* 62, 332–52; Leeds, E.T. (1922), 'Further discoveries of the Neolithic and Bronze Ages at Peterborough', *Antiquaries Journal,* 2, 220–37. Hawkes, C.F.C. and Fell, C.I. (1945), 'The Early Iron Age settlement at Fengate, Peterborough', *Archaeological Journal,* 100, 188–223. Smith, I.F. (1956), *The decorative art of Neolithic ceramics in south-eastern England, and its relations,* Ph.D. thesis, Institute of Archaeology, London University. Royal Commission on Historical Monuments (England) (1968), *Peterborough New Town: a Survey of the Antiquities in the areas of Development,* H.M.S.O., London.

Two reports on our recent work a few miles north of Peterborough: Pryor, F.M.M. and French, C.A.I. (1986), *The Fenland Project Number 1: Archaeology and Environment in the Lower Welland Valley,* 2 vols. East Anglian Archaeology, 27, Cambridge. Pryor, F.M.M., French, C.A.I. and Taylor, M. (1986), 'An interim report on excavations at Etton, Maxey, Cambridgeshire, 1982–1984', *Antiquaries Journal,* 65, 275–311.

3   The first farmers (4000–2000 BC)

The archaeology of context is well covered in these collected case studies: Kinnes, I.A. and Barrett, J.C. (1989), *The Archaeology of Context in the Neolithic and Bronze Age: Recent Trends,* Department of Archaeology, Sheffield University.

Good examples of detailed regional studies: Louwe-Kooijmans, L.P. (1974), 'The Rhine/Meuse Delta: four studies on its prehistoric occupation and Holocene geology', *Analecta Praehistorica Leidensia,* 8, Leiden; Fleming, A. (1988), *The Dartmoor Reaves: investigating prehistoric land divisions,* Batsford, London; Coles, J.M. and others (1975–1988), *Somerset Levels Papers,* Annual collection of papers published by the Somerset Levels Project, Taunton.

The Wilsford shaft (a chalkland Bronze Age well): Ashbee, P., Bell, M. and Proudfoot, E. (1989), *Wilsford Shaft: Excavations 1960–62,* English Heritage Archaeological Report no. 11, London.

Archaeology in the Avebury region, an excellent contrast with the present volume: Malone,

C. (1989), *English Heritage book of Avebury,* Batsford/English Heritage, London.

The effects of radiocarbon dating on archaeological thought, an early view: Renfrew, A.C. (1973), *Before Civilization,* Cape, London.

A new and controversial view of the spread of Indo-European languages across Europe: Renfrew, A.C. (1987), *Archaeology and Language,* Cape, London 1987; Penguin Books, Harmondsworth, 1989.

The conventional view of Indo-European language spread: Mallory, J.P. (1989), *In Search of the Indo-Europeans: Language, Archaeology and Myth,* Thames and Hudson, London.

The Neolithic period – the most recent text: Whittle, A.W.R. (1988), *Problems in Neolithic Archaeology,* New Studies in Archaeology, Cambridge University Press.

A view of the earliest Neolithic in the north European 'fringe': Madsen, T., and Jensen, H.J. (1982), 'Settlement and Land Use in Early Neolithic Denmark', *Analecta Praehistorica Leidensia,* 15, 64–86.

The earliest Neolithic landscape in Fengate, and its significance: Pryor, F.M.M. (1988), 'Earlier Neolithic organised landscapes and ceremonial in lowland Britain' in Barrett, J.C., and Kinnes, I.A. (eds.) *The Archaeology of Context in the Neolithic and Bronze Age: Recent Trends,* 63–72, Dept. Archaeology and Prehistory, Sheffield University.

The clearance of woodland in the Mesolithic Fenland: 'Mesolithic and Neolithic activity and environmental impact on the south-east fen-edge in Cambridgeshire', *Proceedings of the Prehistoric Society,* 55, 207–50.

Probably the best study of a Neolithic region: Louwe-Kooijmans, L.P. (1974), 'The Rhine Meuse Delta', *Analecta Praehistorica Leidensia,* 7.

For comparisons of Dutch and English Neolithic pottery: Louwe-Kooijmans, L.P. (1976), 'Local development in a borderland', *Oudheidkundige Mededelingen uit het Rijkmuseum van Oudheded te Leiden,* 57, 227–297.

Bronze Age contacts across the North Sea: O'Connor, B. (1980), *Cross-Channel Relations in the later Bronze Age,* British Archaeological Reports International Series, No. 91, 2 vols., Oxford.

Fengate site 11, the full report: Pryor, F.M.M. (forthcoming), 'Excavations at Site 11, Fengate, 1969' in Simpson, W.G., Gurney, D.A., Neve, J. and Pryor, F.M.M. *Excavations in Peterborough and the Lower Welland Valley, 1961–1969,* Fenland Project Monograph, East Anglian Archaeology.

A closely similar site to Fengate Site 11: Buckley, D.G., Major, H. and Milton, B. (1988), 'Excavation of a possible Neolithic long barrow or mortuary enclosure at Rivenhall, Essex, 1986', *Proceedings of the Prehistoric Society,* 54, 77–92.

4 The earlier Bronze Age (2000–1000 BC)

The scale of East Anglian co-axial field systems can be extensive; these examples are of Iron Age date: Williamson, T. (1987), 'Early co-axial field systems on the East Anglian boulder clays', *Proceedings of the Prehistoric Society,* 53, 419–32.

A vivid reconstruction of life on a British Iron Age farm, based on practical experience: Reynolds, P.J. (1979), *Iron-Age Farm: the Butser Experiment,* British Museum, London.

For the Fenland Project in general: Hall, D. and others (1988), 'Survey environment and excavation in the English Fenland', *Antiquity,* 62, 305–80.

For an introduction to barrows, by a pioneer in the field: Grinsell, L.V. (1979), *Barrows in England and Wales,* Shire Archaeology, Shire Books, Princes Risborough.

Ashbee's Round and Long barrow books, although out-dated, are still essential: Ashbee, P. (1960), *The Bronze Age Round Barrow in Britain,* Phoenix House, London; Ashbee, P. (1970), *The Earthen Long Barrow in Britain,* Dent, London.

We now know that round barrows may sometimes be Neolithic: Kinnes, I.A. (1979), *Round Barrows and Ring-Ditches in the British Neolithic,* Dept. of Prehistoric and Romano-British Antiquities, Occasional Paper, No. 7, The British Museum, London.

For buried Fenland barrowfields: Hall, D.N. (1987), 'Regional Fieldwork on the Wash Fenlands of England' in Coles, J.M. and Lawson, A.J. (eds) *European Wetlands in Prehistory,* 169–80, Oxford University Press.

The Haddenham Fenland long barrow has proved particularly exciting: Shand, P. and Hodder, I.R. (1990), 'Haddenham', *Current Archaeology,* 10, 339–42.

The contrast between Wessex and East Anglia in the Neolithic: Pryor, F.M.M. (1984), 'Personalities of Britain: two examples of long-term regional contrast', *Scottish Archaeological*

Review, 3, 8–15.

5 *The later Bronze Age (1000–700 BC)*
For soils, snails and other environmental topics, and their roles in archaeology, with many references: Evans, J.G. (1978), *An Introduction to Environmental Archaeology,* Paul Elek, London.

The Flag Fen wood specialist's own introduction to the subject: Taylor, M. (1981), *Wood in Archaeology,* Shire Books, Princes Risborough.

A superbly preserved early Iron Age house in Holland: Therkhorn, L.L., Brandt, R.W., Pals, J.P. and Taylor, M. (1984), 'An early Iron Age farmstead: Site Q of the Assendelver Polders project', *Proceedings of the Prehistoric Society,* 50, 351–74.

A suggested reconstruction of timbers at Flag Fen: Taylor, M. and Pryor, F.M.M. (1990), 'Bronze Age building techniques at Flag Fen, Peterborough, England', *World Archaeology,* 21, 425–34.

'Fenland rapiers' of the Middle Bronze Age were amongst the earliest items in Britain to be deliberately thrown into water: Trump, B.A.V. (1968), 'Fenland Rapiers' in Coles, J.M. and Simpson, D.D.A. (eds) *Studies in Ancient Europe,* 213–26, Leicester University Press.

Experimental archaeology is a field of growing importance: Coles, J.M. (1973), *Archaeology by Experiment,* Hutchinson, London.

Middle Bronze Age Fenland metalwork in its wider context: Rowlands, M.J. (1976). *The production and distribution of metalwork in the Middle Bronze Age in southern Britain,* British Archaeological Reports No. 31, 2 vols., Oxford.

For Bronze Age helmets: Hencken, H. (1971), *The earliest European helmets,* American School of Prehistoric Research Bulletin 28, Peabody Museum, Harvard University.

The largest Bronze Age hoard yet found in Britain: Britton, D. (1960), 'The Isleham hoard, Cambridgeshire', *Antiquity,* 34, 279–82.

The Caergwrle bowl: Savory, H.N. (1980), *Guide Catalogue of the Bronze Age Collections,* National Museum of Wales, Cardiff.

An excellent overview of wetland archaeology: Coles, B.J. and J.M. (1989), *People of the Wetlands,* Thames and Hudson, London.

Two stimulating reviews of British prehistory: Bradley, R.J. (1978), *The Prehistoric Settlement of Britain,* Routledge and Kegan Paul, London. Bradley, R.J. (1984), *The Social Foundations of Prehistoric Britain,* Longman, London.

The same author has just published a review of Bronze Age ceremonial, very relevant to Flag Fen: Bradley, R.J. (1990), *The Passage of Arms,* Cambridge University Press.

Communities assert their own identities in times of tension, especially at territorial boundaries: Hodder, I.R. (1982), *Symbols in Action,* Cambridge University Press.

6 *The Iron Age (700 BC–AD 43)*
The standard text on the British Iron Age: Cunliffe, B.W. (1978), *Iron Age Communities in Britain,* 2nd ed., Routledge, London.

Burial in the Iron Age took a variety of forms: Whimster, R. (1977), 'Iron Age Burial in Southern Britain', *Proceedings of the Prehistoric Society,* 43, 317–28.

The Roman Fen Causeway or Great Fen Road is treated in detail in: Phillips, C.W. (1970), *The Fenland in Roman Times,* Royal Geographical Society, Research Series, No. 5, London.

Glossary

alluviation The process whereby *alluvium* is laid down. Alluvium is fine-grained, sticky clay which is deposited by rivers, usually in winter, in times of flood.

awl (or bradawl) A small pointed implement, usually in metal, used to make holes, but without a drilling action.

Bronze Age Follows the Neolithic, from *c.*1800–700 BC, and sees the adoption of metal-working: first of copper, then of bronze (an alloy mainly of copper, with tin, and sometimes lead too).

coppicing Certain trees and shrubs can be cut back at regular intervals to provide long, thin and straight poles or rods. If this is done at ground level it is termed coppicing, and the gnarled wood from which the shoots grow is known as a coppice 'stool' (see also **pollarding**).

Cretaceous The third and last age of reptiles (dinosaurs), 140–65 million years ago. The chalk hills of England date to this period (see also **Jurassic**).

dendrochronology The study of tree-rings as a means of providing precise dates. Dendro-chronologists can also provide important information on forest/woodland management and exploitation.

drove A shortening of 'droveway', a road or track specifically intended for driving animals and their herdsmen or drovers. In the Fens droves from drier land into the seasonally available wet pastures were an important feature of the landscape.

Hallstatt A site in Austria that has produced a wealth of early Iron Age and Late Bronze Age metalwork. The typological development of these items is used to provide the chronological framework for the earlier Iron Age of central Europe, from *c.*1200 to *c.*450 BC (see also **La Tène**).

henge Derived from Stonehenge. A class of Late Neolithic (*c.*2000 BC) ceremonial sites involving one or more large circular ditches, sometimes enclosing a setting of posts or stones. They are only found in Britain.

humify To convert into humus, the organic component of the topsoil. In peat lands humification follows swiftly upon drainage. It is a process highly detrimental to organic archaeological deposits.

Iron Age Follows the Bronze Age and sees the widespread adoption of iron as the main tool- and weapon-making metal. Iron smelting requires a sophisticated fire and furnace technology.

Jurassic The great age of reptiles, 195–140 million years ago; in England blue Oxford Clay was laid down in its warm seas (see also **Cretaceous**).

La Tène A small lake in Switzerland in which were found large numbers of Iron Age swords etc. The typological development of these items is used to provide the chronological framework for the later Iron Age of continental Europe, from *c.*450 BC until the Roman Conquest (see also **Hallstatt**).

marine transgression A period when the sea covered large areas of low-lying fen. When the waters retreated we talk of a **regression phase**.

Mesolithic or Middle Stone Age. Follows the Palaeolithic and the last Ice Age. People subsisted on hunting, gathering and fishing and made distinctive fish-spears and arrowheads from very small flakes of flint, known as microliths.

Neolithic or New Stone Age. The period of the first farmers. It follows the Mesolithic and sees the widespread adoption of pottery and stone technologies that involved the use of grinding and polishing.

overburden A general term to describe topsoil or other material that lies over (and conceals) archaeological levels.

Palaeolithic or Old Stone Age. The earliest archaeological period. In Europe the Palaeolithic dates to the Ice Ages, when mankind survived by hunting and gathering wild foods.

palaeosol An ancient soil. They usually survive buried beneath burial mounds, ditch banks etc. In the Fens palaeosols can be found beneath later water-borne deposits of peat and clay.

palstave The main axe type of the Middle Bronze Age. It consists of a flat piece of bronze with raised side-walls and a stop-ridge against which a split shaft is bound. It is not a particularly efficient way of mounting an axe blade.

pollarding Certain trees, especially willows, grow long, straight shoots if they are cut back regularly. Pollards are trees cut back, usually above head height, to keep the young shoots clear of browsing animals (see also **coppicing**).

radiocarbon dating A dating method used on organic materials, such as wood, charcoal or bone. All living things absorb mildly radioactive carbon which breaks down at a uniform rate upon death; this rate of decay can be measured to provide a date.

roddon/rodham An extinct, silt-filled tidal creek bed. Most are of prehistoric age and traverse large tracts of Fenland; they are best seen in peaty soils where the white of the silt contrasts strongly with the dark peats.

sock a countryman's term for the water-table. Sock wells penetrate to the sock, and are usually no more than 2 m (6 ft) deep.

subsoil The material immediately below the topsoil, from which it is partly composed. The nature of the subsoil dictates the type of topsoil that will form on it; thus a clay subsoil gives rise to a heavy topsoil.

turbaries Land set-aside for peat-cutting, usually for fuel.

typology An archaeological system for classifying the chronological development of any given item: thus axe typology sees the development of socketed axes from winged axes (Late Bronze Age) which in turn develop from palstaves (Middle Bronze Age), flanged axes and flat axes (Early Bronze Age). It is a useful technique, but very prone to over-elaboration.

use-life The period when a site or building was actually in use.

Index

(Page numbers in **bold** refer to illustrations)